Editor
Gisela Lee

Editorial Manager
Karen J. Goldfluss, M.S. Ed.

Editor-in-Chief
Sharon Coan, M.S. Ed.

Illustrator
Howard Chaney

Cover Artist
Jessica Orlando

Art Coordinator
Denice Adorno

Creative Director
Elayne Roberts

Imaging
James Edward Grace

Product Manager
Phil Garcia

Publisher
Mary D. Smith, M.S. Ed.

How to Solve Word Problems

Grades 4–5

Author
Charles Shields

Teacher Created Resources, Inc.
6421 Industry Way
Westminster, CA 92683
www.teachercreated.com
ISBN-1-57690-949-2

©2000 Teacher Created Resources, Inc.
Reprinted, 2005
Made in U.S.A.

The classroom teacher may reproduce copies of materials in this book for classroom use only. The reproduction of any part for an entire school or school system is strictly prohibited. No part of this publication may be transmitted, stored, or recorded in any form without written permission from the publisher.

Table of Contents

 © Teacher Created Resources, Inc.

A Note to Teachers and Parents

Welcome to the "How to" math series! You have chosen one of over two dozen books designed to give your children the information and practice they need to acquire important concepts in specific areas of math. The goal of the "How to" math books is to give children an extra boost as they work toward mastery of the math skills established by the National Council of Teachers of Mathematics (NCTM) and outlined in grade-level scope and sequence guidelines.

The design of this book is intended to allow it to be used by teachers or parents for a variety of purposes and needs. Each of the units contains one "How to" page and at least one practice page. The "How to" section of each unit precedes the practice pages and provides needed information such as a concept or math rule review, important terms and formulas to remember, or step-by-step guidelines necessary for using the practice pages. While most "How to" pages are written for direct use by the children, in some lower-grade-level books these pages are presented as instructional pages or direct lessons to be used by a teacher or parent prior to introducing the practice pages.

About This Book

The activities in this book will help your children learn new skills or reinforce skills already learned in the following areas:

- solving word problems step by step
- estimating reasonable answers
- recognizing unnecessary, extra information
- solving for more than one answer
- using data on charts and tables to solve word problems

Word problems draw on children's ability to read carefully, think logically, eliminate choices, and devise solutions. Unfortunately, many children dread word problems as "unfair" and "tricky" descriptions of events. In fact, tackling word problems can be a major benefit to students. Not only do word problems sharpen students' mathematical reasoning skills, they also enable students to become better readers and writers. In word problems, the words themselves and the presentation of information, are critically important. Word problems teach youngsters that how a problem is stated and the way the facts are told make a difference in understanding. Every good writer knows this, and every thoughtful reader learns to appreciate it.

How to Solve Word Problems: Grades 4–5 presents a comprehensive, step-by-step overview of how to analyze information in a word problem with clear, simple, readable instructional activities. The 12 units in this book can be used in whole-class instruction with the teacher or by a parent assisting his or her child with the concepts and exercises. This book also lends itself to use by small groups doing remedial or review work on the fundamentals of addition, subtraction, multiplication, or division in solving word problems. Children and small groups in earlier grades who are engaged in enrichment or advanced work will find the units useful, too. Finally, this book can be used in a learning center with materials specified for each unit of instruction.

If children have difficulty on a specific concept or unit in this book, review the material and allow them to redo pages that are difficult for them. Since step-by-step concept development is essential, it's best not to skip sections of the book. Even if children find a unit easy, mastering the problems will build their confidence as they approach more difficult concepts.

Make available simple manipulatives to reinforce concepts. Use pennies, buttons, a ruler, beans, and similar materials to show parts being added or subtracted, for instance. Many children can grasp a numerical concept much easier if they see it demonstrated.

How to Solve Word Problems: Grades 4–5 highlights the NCTM standards that state the study of mathematics should emphasize problem solving in such a way that students can use problem-solving approaches to investigate and understand the general content of mathematics. Students are encouraged to solve problems involving everyday situations and real-life applications of math skills. These specific skills should help students develop strategies to solve a wide variety of math-related problems, to verify the accuracy and results of specific problems, and to acquire facility and confidence in making mathematics a meaningful enterprise for them.

Use every opportunity to have students apply these new skills in classroom situations and at home. This will reinforce the value of the skill as well as the process. This book matches a number of NCTM standards, including these main topics and specific features.

Solving Word Problems Step by Step

Research that extends back to the 1950s indicates that students need to follow four steps to solve word problems: understand the problem, plan the solution, solve the problem, and review the solution. However, this unit takes a slightly different approach that gives students specific things to look for: What does the problem ask you to find? What information is needed to solve the problem? How can you show the problem with numbers? And what is your answer?

Estimating Reasonable Answers

Estimating helps students eliminate unrealistic possibilities right away. "Reasonable" means that the answer can be defended logically. Estimating reasonable answers means that students can stop worrying that there is one "needle in a haystack" answer and instead get on with the thinking that is needed to work the problem out.

Recognizing Unnecessary, Extra Information

Many nonmathematical problems in life have information that is not related to the essential problem. For instance, "Lauren's red car won't start." The color of the car is unimportant. So, too, in word problems, students must recognize when certain information is not needed to find the answer.

Mathematical Connections Among Fractions, Decimals, Percents, and Ratios

The instructions in this book emphasize the connections among ideas in mathematics. Word problems involving fractions, decimals, percents, and ratios reinforce the importance of understanding that a portion of something may be expressed several ways, or determined several ways, without sacrificing accuracy.

Using Data from Graphs to Solve Word Problems

Word problems in life can occur as directions, too, such as "Using the bar graph above, which movie grossed the highest amount of money at the box office in 2000?" This unit poses similar problems which can be answered by reviewing the information in graphs.

Other Standards

This book aligns well with other standards which focus on teaching computational skills, such as division and multiplication within the context of measurement and geometry. Students are also urged to think critically, a skill contained in nearly all local, state, and national standards.

 © Teacher Created Resources, Inc.

1 How to • • • • • • • • • • • • • Approach Word Problems

Facts to Know

To solve word problems, most students find it helpful if they answer four questions:

- What does the problem ask you to find?
- What information is needed to solve the problem?
- How can you show the problem with numbers?
- What is your answer?

What Does the Problem Ask You to Find?

Think about this: you might not completely understand a word problem and still solve it. What if a problem asked, "If 2 perflibbets and 3 tungonnies shared a ride to the fair, and each sat in only one seat, how many seats were used?" You don't know what perflibbets or tungonnies are, but would you be able to choose the correct answer?

(A) 4 (B) 5 (C) 3 (D) 2

If you chose (B) 5, you're right!

All that is needed to start thinking about an answer is to recognize what is asked for. The following buzzwords can help you recognize this information:

• what	• how many	• which
• what time	• how far	• which one
• at what time	• how long	• find
• how	• who	• determine
• how much		

Usually, what the problem is asking you to find is described in the last sentence of the problem, and it's worded as a question.

Sample

Mr. Silverman offered to drive everyone to the football game at the University of Illinois. The distance is 90 miles. How long will it take him to get there traveling 60 mph?

It's often very helpful to look back at the last sentence as you try to solve the problem.

What Information Is Needed to Solve the Problem?

The first step in recognizing what information is needed is to recognize what kind of word problem you're going to solve. Here are the basic kinds:

- **Percent Problems**

  15 is 30% of what number?

  What percent is 8 of 17?

- **Number Problems**

  The sum of 2 consecutive integers is 15. What are the integers?

  3 times more than some number is 27. What is the number?

Approach Word Problems

Facts to Know

What Information Is Needed to Solve the Problem? *(cont.)*

- **Money Problems**

  You have 13 coins totaling $2.75 in your pocket. They are all quarters and dimes. How many of each type of coin do you have?

- **Ratio Problems**

  The ratio of people with long hair to short hair is 3:2. There are 66 people with long hair. How many short-haired people are there?

- **Age Problems**

  Angela is 10 years old. Manuel is 21 years old. In how many years will Angela be 3 times as old as Manuel is now?

- **Mixture Problems**

  Walnuts cost $1.75 per pound and peanuts cost $2.20 per pound. How many of each should be used to create a five-pound mixture that costs $3.20 per pound?

- **Rate Problems**

  A ship goes downstream for 4 hours, turns around, and takes 6 hours to get back upstream. The water in the stream is moving at 3 mph. How fast was the ship going coming back upstream?

Figure out whether you are looking for an answer that will be a percent, a number, an amount of money, a ratio, a rate, a number of years, or a total of two or more mixtures. This will make you focus on information connected to the answer.

How Can You Show the Problem with Numbers?

A word problem is actually a math expression, only the expression is "buried" inside the description. You need to bring the math expression out of the description.

Sample

A baker can bake 5 cakes an hour. He worked for 2 hours, but he was a little tired, so he made 2 fewer than usual. How many cakes did he make?

As a math expression, this problem looks like this:
(2 x 5) – 2 = ?

How to Approach Word Problems

Writers of word problems often start with the math expression and then write a word problem to fit the expression.

You could write: Some volunteers were needed at school to help paint the scenes for the play. First, three students showed up and then seven more. "Oh, that's twice as many painting scenes as we need painting scenes," said Mrs. Owens. How many students did she need painting scenes?

What Is Your Answer?

A key word in checking the answer to any math problem is "reasonable." Your answer should be reasonable given the facts. In other words, you should be able to explain your answer in a logical way. Now and then, try explaining your answer to yourself as if you were helping a classmate who didn't understand the problem. Play teacher to yourself—it works!

 © Teacher Created Resources, Inc.

1 Practice • • • • • • • • • Solving Simple Word Problems

Directions: Using the information on pages 5 and 6, solve the following word problems.

1. There were 1,622 students at James Hart High School. If 40 students moved away, how many were left?

Step #1: What does the problem ask you to find?

a. how many students moved away
b. how many students were at the high school
c. how many students were left
d. how many students were in the school altogether

Step #2: What information is needed to solve the problem?

e. number of students in the high school
f. initial number of students and the number of students who moved away
g. number of students who will be in the school next year
h. number of students who were in the school last year

Step #3: How can you show the problem with numbers?

i. 1,622 – 40
j. 1,622 x 40
k. 1,622 ÷ 40
l. 1,622 + 40

Step #4: What's your answer?

m. 1,582
n. 405
o. 40.55
p. 1,662

2. Mr. Webb has been collecting gems for 3 years. His favorite gems are rubies. Out of his 233 gems, 75 are rubies. How many gems does he have that are not rubies, if there are 3 other types of gemstones?

Step #1: What does the problem ask you to find?

a. number of gems he has that are not rubies
b. number of gems he has that are rubies
c. number of gems he collects each year
d. number of other types of gems that he owns

Step #2: What information is needed to solve the problem?

e. total number of gems and number of rubies
f. number of years
g. number of gems that are not rubies
h. total number of gems he owns

Step #3: How can you show the problem with numbers?

i. 233 – (75 + 3)
j. 233 – 75
k. 233 + 75
l. 75 – 233

Step #4: What is your answer?

m. 258 gems
n. 75 gems
o. 158 gems
p. 168 gems

3. It took Charley $1\frac{1}{2}$ hours to make a birdhouse. It took him twice as long to make a doghouse. It took him three times as long to make a bike rack. How long did he need to make a birdhouse and a doghouse for his Aunt Maude?

Step #1: What does the problem ask you to find?

a. number of hours he needs to make a birdhouse
b. number of hours he needs to make a doghouse
c. number of hours he needs to make a birdhouse and a doghouse
d. number of hours it took him to make a bike rack

Step #2: What information is needed to solve the problem?

e. number of hours it takes to make a birdhouse
f. number of hours it takes to make a doghouse
g. number of hours it takes to make a birdhouse and a doghouse
h. number of hours it takes to make a bike rack

Step #3: How can you show the problem with numbers?

i. $1\frac{1}{2} + (2 \times 1\frac{1}{2}) + (3 \times 1\frac{1}{2})$
j. $1\frac{1}{2} + (2 \times 1\frac{1}{2})$
k. $1\frac{1}{2} + (3 \times 1\frac{1}{2})$
l. $(2 \times 1\frac{1}{2}) + (3 \times 1\frac{1}{2})$

Step #4: What is your answer?

m. 9 hours
n. $4\frac{1}{2}$ hours
o. 6 hours
p. $7\frac{1}{2}$ hours

 © Teacher Created Resources, Inc.

2 How to • • • • • • • • • • Solve Multiple-Step Problems

Facts to Know

You may need to use more than one operation to solve some problems. These are called multiple-step problems. But before you start these multiple-step problems, keep in mind that you need to ask yourself these four important questions:

- What does the problem ask you to find?
- What information is needed to solve the problem?
- How can you show the problem with numbers?
- What is your answer?

Sample A

The jeweler can make 6 rings in two days. How many rings could he make in 9 days?

Hint: *You need to know how many rings he can make in one day.*

First, divide 6 (rings) by 2 to see how many rings he could make in one day.

6 ÷ 2 = 3

Second, multiply your answer (3) by 9 to see how many rings he could make in 9 days.

3 x 9 = 27 rings in 9 days

The jeweler can make 27 rings in 9 days.

Sample B

The donut shop baker makes 1 dozen donuts every 15 minutes. How many donuts can the baker make in 1 hour?

Hint: *Remember that there are 60 minutes in an hour and 1 dozen donuts = 12 donuts.*

First, divide 60 (minutes) by 15 to see how many 15-minute intervals make up 1 hour.

60 ÷ 15 = 4

Second, multiply your answer (4) by 12 to see how many donuts the baker can make in 1 hour.

4 x 12 = 48 donuts in 1 hour

The baker can make 48 donuts in 1 hour.

Sample C

Michelle gets $5.00 as a weekly allowance. She is saving her money to buy her mother a birthday gift. If Michelle saves her money for 35 days, how much money will she have saved to buy her mother a gift?

Hint: *Remember 7 days = 1 week.*

First, divide 35 (days) by 7 to see how many weeks Michelle saved her money.

35 ÷ 7 = 5

Second, multiply your answer (5) by $5.00 to see how much money Michelle saved to buy her mother a birthday gift.

5 x $5.00 = $25.00

Michelle saved $25.00 to buy her mother a birthday gift.

2 Practice • • • • • • • Solving Multiple-Step Problems

Directions: Using the information on page 9, solve the problems below and on pages 11 and 12.

In the first year of production, the James Hart High School theater sold 1,572 tickets. In its second year, it sold 1,753 tickets. In its third year, it sold 152 fewer than in its second year. How many tickets were sold in 3 years?

1. What does the problem ask you to find?

a. how long the theater has been around

b. how many tickets were sold the third year

c. how many tickets were sold in 3 years

d. which year was the best year for selling tickets

2. What information is needed to solve the problem?

Hint: *First, find out how many tickets were sold the third year—that's the missing information. Then you can find out how many were sold for three years.*

3. How can you show the problem with numbers?

e. 1,572 + 1,753 + 152 =

f. 1,572 + 1,753 – 152 =

g. 1,572 + 1,753 + 152 x 3 =

h. 1,572 + 1,753 + (1,753 –152) =

4. What is your answer?

i. 1,601

j. 4,926

k. 1,753

l. 4,332

Some students are holding a bake sale to raise money for their school library. They are selling fudge, peanut butter squares, and cookies. One of each type of treat is put into 95 paper bags. The kids decided they would keep the leftovers. They started out with 130 pieces of fudge, 116 peanut butter squares, and 110 cookies. How much did they get to keep after dividing the treats?

5. What does the problem ask you to find?

a. how many treats they sold in total

b. how many bags they used for each treat

c. which treat had the most left over

d. how many treats they get to keep after dividing and placing them in the paper bags

6. What information is needed to solve the problem?

e. how many of each treat went into each bag

f. how many bags is 3 x 95

g. how much of each treat is left over after subtracting 95

h. how much is 110 from 116 and from 130

7. How can you show the problem with numbers?

Hint: *You must find three separate answers because there are three treats of different amounts, but one number is constant—95 bags. So subtract 95 from the total number of each type of treat.*

8. What is your answer?

i. 95 pieces of each

j. 15 cookies, 35 pieces of fudge, 21 peanut butter squares

k. $22\frac{1}{2}$ of each

l. $31\frac{2}{3}$ of each

© Teacher Created Resources, Inc.

2 Practice • • • • • • • Solving Multiple-Step Problems

One morning, a grasshopper fell down a hole 2 meters deep. He would climb $\frac{1}{4}$ of a meter every day, but at night he would slide down $\frac{1}{8}$ of a meter. At this rate, how many days until the grasshopper got out?

9. What does the problem ask you to find?

a. how far the grasshopper slides down from 2 meters

b. what is $\frac{1}{4} \times \frac{1}{8}$

c. what is $2 \times \frac{1}{4} \times 8$

d. how many days total

10. What information is needed to solve the problem?

e. how much he goes up every day

f. how much he slides down every night

g. what is the difference between $\frac{1}{4}$ up and $\frac{1}{8}$ down each day

h. how deep is 2 meters

11. How can you show the problem with numbers?

Hint: *Find how much actual progress the grasshopper makes every day. Then write a division problem that shows how many days, at $\frac{1}{8}$ of a meter per day, it would take until he is at 1.75 meters. (Remember, on the last day he only has $\frac{1}{4}$ meter to go!)*

12. What is your answer?

i. 2 meters

j. 15 days

k. 14 days

l. 8 days

On an average day, Californians spend $958,904 buying gasoline and groceries. Of this total $767,123 is spent on gasoline. In one week, how much do Californians spend on groceries?

13. What does the problem ask you to find?

a. how much is spent on groceries in a day

b. how much is spent on groceries in a week

c. how much is spent on gasoline in a day

d. what is the weekly amount spent on groceries

14. What information is needed to solve the problem?

Hint: *You need to know the difference between the amount spent on gasoline and food in a week to determine how much is spent on groceries only?*

15. How can you show the problem with numbers?

e. $958,904 – $767,123 =

f. 7 x $958,904 – $767,123 =

g. $958,904 + $767,123 x 7 =

h. ($958,904 – $767,123) x 7 =

16. What is your answer?

i. $1,342,467

j. $12,081,989

k. $5,369,861

l. $6,712,328

2 Practice •••••••• Solving Multiple-Step Problems

Directions: Answer the questions to solve each problem.

17. A manufacturer claims that a new motor oil saves 5 percent of the gasoline used by a car. If a person drives 24,000 kilometers a year and he or she gets 32 kilometers per gallon of gasoline, how many gallons of gasoline could he or she save in one year?

Hint: *First, you need to know how many gallons you're using in a year.*

- What does the problem ask you to find? ____________________
- What information is needed to solve the problem? ____________________
- How can you show the problem with numbers? ____________________
- What is your answer? ____________________

18. Grandpa Todd bought a 5-pound block of cheese. The cheese was divided equally among 8 families at a picnic. How many ounces of cheese did each family get?

Hint: *You need to convert the 5 pounds into ounces first.*

- What does the problem ask you to find? ____________________
- What information is needed to solve the problem? ____________________
- How can you show the problem with numbers? ____________________
- What is your answer? ____________________

19. Jessica has a bet with Lauren. She says no one could live to be a billion seconds old. Lauren says that's not so old—big deal! How old in years is a billion seconds?

Hint: *Go step by step to change seconds into minutes, minutes into hours, hours into days, and days into years.*

- What does the problem ask you to find? ____________________
- What information is needed to solve the problem? ____________________
- How can you show the problem with numbers? ____________________
- What is your answer? ____________________

20. A gardener can plant 28 seedlings in 40 minutes. How many can he plant in 1 hour and 10 minutes?

Hint: *First, find out how many seedlings can be planted in a minute.*

- What does the problem ask you to find? ____________________
- What information is needed to solve the problem? ____________________
- How can you show the problem with numbers? ____________________
- What is your answer? ____________________

© Teacher Created Resources, Inc.

3 How to • • • • • Work Backwards Toward Answers

Facts to Know

To solve some problems, you may need to undo the key actions in the problem. This strategy is called working backwards. But before you start these problems, keep in mind that you need to ask yourself these four important questions:

- *What does the problem ask you to find?*
- *What information is needed to solve the problem?*
- *How can you show the problem with numbers?*
- *What is your answer?*

Sample A

The bakers at Slice o' Pie Restaurant ate 4 pies that were left over from work on Thursday night. 12 pies were sold at the restaurant that night. The manager took 2 home with her after work. How many pies were at the restaurant Thursday night?

First, find out the total number of pies sold or taken home.

12 pies sold + 2 pies taken home = 14 pies

Next, add back the 4 pies that the bakers ate.

14 pies sold or taken home + 4 pies eaten by the bakers = 18 pies

Therefore, there were 18 pies at Slice o' Pie Restaurant Thursday night.

Sample B

Marta likes to borrow books from the library. She borrowed 18 books over a 3-month period of time (January-March). If Marta borrowed 8 books in January and 6 books in February, how many books did she borrow in March?

Subtract the number of books Marta borrowed in January and February from the total number of books to determine how many she borrowed in March.

18 books – 8 books – 6 books = 4 books

Marta borrowed 4 books in March.

Finding Solutions by Working Backwards

Directions: Using the information on page 13, solve the problems below and on pages 15 and 16. Some of the problems provide hints to help you solve them.

Grace has to be at work by 9:00 A.M. It takes her 15 minutes to get dressed, 20 minutes to eat, and 35 minutes to walk to work. What time should she get up?

1. What does the problem ask you to find?

a. what's the total time it takes her to get ready

b. how far away is work

c. what time does she have to be at work

d. what time should she get up

2. What information is needed to solve the problem?

e. what time does she get to work

f. what's the sum of (15 + 20 + 35) minutes

g. what's the difference between 9:00 A.M. and the sum of (15 + 20 + 35) minutes

h. what's the total sum of 9:00 A.M. and the sum of (15 + 20 + 35) minutes

3. How can you show the problem with numbers?

Hint: *Write a problem that shows working backward from 9:00 A.M. by subtracting the time Grace spent doing other activites to calculate what time she got up.*

4. What is your answer?

i. 10:35 A.M.

j. 8:10 A.M.

k. 7:30 A.M.

l. 7:50 A.M.

Mr. Hall asked his students to open their math books to the facing pages whose page numbers add up to 85. To which pages should the children turn?

5. What does the problem ask you to find?

a. what is page 85

b. how to open the math book to facing pages

c. what are the facing pages whose page numbers add up to 85

d. how many students opened their books to page 85

6. What information is needed to solve the problem?

e. how many tries will it take to get 85

f. what is 1 x 85

g. what is 84 + 86

h. what is about half of 85

7. How can you show the problem with numbers?

Hint: *You know the total already. The numbers of two facing pages that total 85 must be around half. Try dividing by two, but remember that page numbers are whole numbers that increase from lowest to highest.*

8. What is your answer?

i. 84 + 86

j. 40 + 45

k. 41 + 44

l. 42 + 43

© Teacher Created Resources, Inc.

Finding Solutions by Working Backwards

Kyle played the same game with Mr. Hall. "I'm thinking of two facing pages that total 127, Mr. Hall," he said. Kyle is thinking of which two facing pages?

9. What does the problem ask you to find?

a. what totals 127

b. what game are Kyle and Mr. Hall playing

c. what is half of 127

d. what are the page numbers of two facing pages that add up to 127

10. What information is needed to solve the problem?

e. how many tries will it take to get 127

f. what is 1 x 127

g. what is 126 + 128

h. what is about half of 127

11. How can you show the problem with numbers?

i. 127 – 1 =

j. (127 – 1) + (127 +1) =

k. 127 ÷ 2 =

l. 127 x 2 =

12. What is your answer?

m. 62 + 63

n. 63 + 64

o. 65 + 66

p. 64 + 65

Felicia passed around a basket of strawberries to the girls at her party. Before the party she ate 5 strawberries and gave a friend 3. Then 8 girls arrived at the party. The first girl took a strawberry, the second girl took 3 strawberries, the third girl took 5 strawberries and so on. After the last girl took her strawberries, the basket was empty. How many strawberries were in the basket at the beginning?

13. What does the problem ask you to find?

a. how many strawberries each girl ate

b. how many strawberries were in the basket at the beginning

c. how many strawberries were eaten before the party

d. how many girls were at the party

14. What information is needed to solve the problem?

Hint: *You need to find the total when eight girls were taking two more strawberries than the previous girl each time. Then you can add back in the 8 that were taken before the party.*

15. How can you show the problem with numbers?

e. 8 x 8 =

f. (1 + 3 + 5) x 8 =

g. 8 x 2 + 8 =

h. 1 + 3 + 5 + 7 + 9 + 11 + 13 + 15 + (3 + 5) =

16. What is your answer?

i. 128

j. 64

k. 72

l. 17

Finding Solutions by Working Backwards

In Wisconsin the Washington Island, ferryboat is full when it has 10 cars on board. It is also full when it has six trucks on board. The ferryboat never carries cars and trucks at the same time.

The ferryboat made five trips across the channel and was full on each trip. It ferried a total of 42 cars and trucks across.

How many cars did the ferryboat carry altogether in the five trips?

17. What does the problem ask you to find?

a. how many cars and trucks went across

b. how many cars and trucks can the ferryboat take at the same time

c. how many trucks went in five trips

d. how many cars went in five trips

18. What information is needed to solve the problem?

e. how many trucks went across in how many trips

f. how many trucks can go in five trips

g. what's the difference between 50 cars and 30 trucks

h. why doesn't the ferry carry cars and trucks at the same time

19. How can you show the problem with numbers?

i. 30 cars + 12 trucks

j. (5 x 6 cars) + (6 x 12 trucks)

k. 5 x 10 cars

l. 32 cars + 10 trucks

20. What is your answer?

m. 50 cars

n. 12 cars

o. 30 cars

p. 42 cars

 © Teacher Created Resources, Inc.

Estimate

Facts to Know

When an exact answer is not needed, you can estimate. There are five ways to estimate.

Front-End Estimate

With this first method of finding the estimate, you will add the front-end digits in each number.

Sample A

Manny collects baseball cards for four teams. He has 42 Chicago White Sox, 86 St. Louis Cardinals, 13 Houston Astros, and 61 New York Yankees. About how many baseball cards does Manny have in his collection?

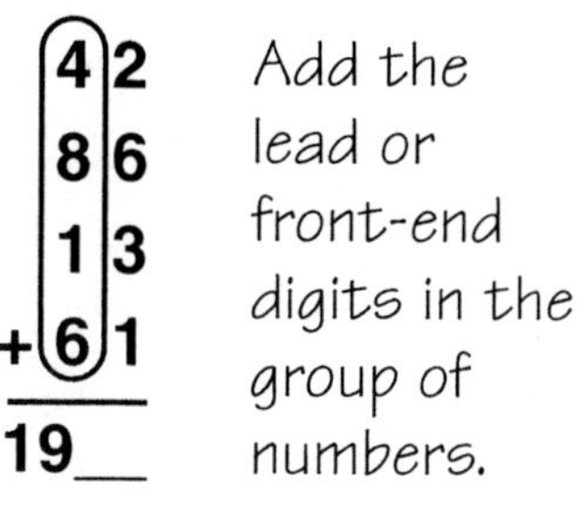

So Manny has about 190 baseball cards in his collection.

Compatible Numbers

When you estimate using compatible numbers, you do "mental math" in your head by looking for numbers that are easy to add. Using this second method of estimating, look at the sample problem discussed above in a different way.

42, 86, 13, 61

86 + 13 ~ 100

42 + 61 ~ 100

100 + 100 = 200

~ is the symbol for "about equal to"

By using compatible numbers and mental math, you estimate that Manny has about 200 baseball cards.

Guess and Check

With this third way of estimating, you will guess or approximate and check your answer.

Sample B

Ian divided 15 games into two piles: the games he owns and the games his brother, Danny, owns. Ian owns 3 more games than Danny. How many games does Danny own?

It's possible to work out a math expression for this problem, but you can also jump right in and guess and check, too.
Let's guess Danny owns 8 games.
That means Ian owns 11 games. That's a total of 19 games.
That guess is too high.
Well, let's guess Danny owns 6 games.
That means Ian owns 9 games. That's a total of 15 games.
That guess is right.
Danny owns 6 games.

Facts to Know

Finding a Range

With this fourth way of estimating, you will find a range for your answer.

Sample C

There were 845 spectators for the sophomore football game at noon on Saturday. Then there were 683 at 2:00 P.M. for the varsity game. What was the range for the attendance on Saturday for both games?

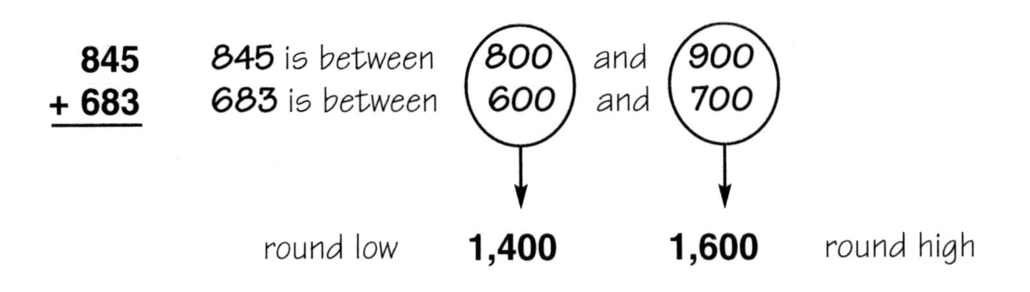

So, the range of attendance was between 1,400–1,600.

Rounding

A fifth strategy is to estimate by rounding each number before adding or subtracting.

Sample D

Eli is on the Buckaroo Bowling Team at Glenwood Bowl. The scores for his first three games were 78, 97, and 126. Estimate the difference between his highest score and his lowest score.

$$\begin{array}{r} 126 \\ -\ 78 \\ \hline \end{array} \xrightarrow{\text{round to the nearest ten}} \begin{array}{r} 130 \\ -\ 80 \\ \hline 50 \end{array}$$

So the estimated difference is 50.

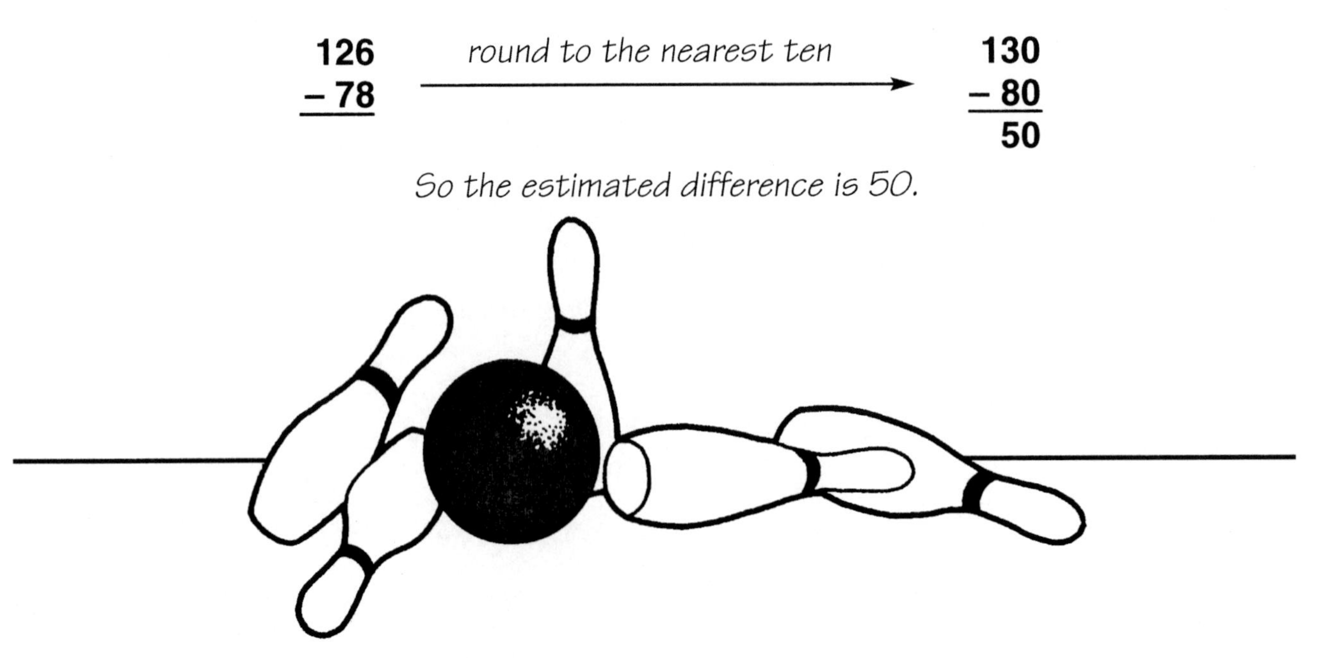

 © Teacher Created Resources, Inc.

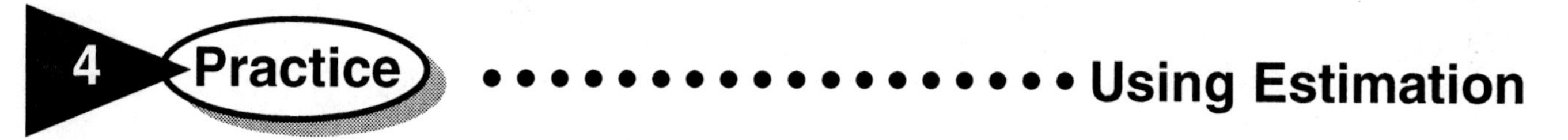

Directions: Using the information on pages 17 and 18, solve the estimation word problems below and on page 20.

1. Lupe, Gloria, and Sylvia went to Texas for a vacation. On the way to Texas, the plane made the trip in 315 minutes. On the return trip, the flight took 216 minutes. Rounding to the nearest 10, how long did the trip there and back take? ____________

2. If 635 people signed up for the three-mile race at 7:30 A.M., and 473 people signed up for the six-mile race at 8:00 A.M. What is the range of how many people entered the races? ____________

3. Fiona was counting tickets quickly to get an estimate of how many people were at the basketball game. In four piles, there were 89, 12, 72, and 26 tickets. She knew almost immediately the first two numbers of the total were about 18. Which method did she use? ____________

4. Todd was working at the Frankfort hardware store and counting sales of patio bricks to get a total. "Just give me an estimate," said his boss. In four sales there were 52 + 18 + 77 + 49. Todd thought to himself, "About 70 and 130 makes . . . 200." He told his boss, "We sold around 200." Which method did he use? ____________

5. Rawlins Farms needs two used trucks for hauling. George Rawlins phoned Steve's Farm Equipment. George told Steve what he needed. Steve knew he had a used truck priced at $4,132 and another one at $5,768. George said, "Just give me a range of what I'm probably going to spend for the two trucks you have." What should Steve say? ____________

6. Henry, April, and Felicia went bowling. Here are their scores:

Bowler	First Game	Second Game
Henry	**124**	**118**
April	**94**	**117**
Felicia	**128**	**132**

a. If you round to the nearest 10, is the estimated difference between April's first-game score and Henry's first-game score greater than or less than 25? ____________

b. Round to the nearest 10 to estimate the total score of each bowler.
Henry ____________ April ____________ Felica ____________

c. Which two bowlers have about a 50-point difference in their total scores?
____

d. In the next alley over, Duane had about 250 total points for two games. If his first-game score ranged from 130–135, what are the lowest and highest scores he might have bowled in the second game? ____________

7. There were 920 tickets sold for the concert in the gym. If 186 people didn't come according to tickets collected at the door, about how many people were in the gym at the concert? (Round all numbers to the nearest ten.) ____________

8. Byron's Bike Shop has two mountain bikes for sale. One costs $434.87, and the other costs $647.90. Byron tells Bob, his salesman, "I don't have price tags on them. If someone wants both bikes, just stay within a decent range." Bob says, "Well, give me a range." What's the range? ____________

This is the table of how many parking spaces were used during baseball season at:

Flosswood Park

	Week 1	Week 2	Week 3	Week 4	Week 5
Parking Spaces Used	325	412	629	685	879

9. Mr. O'Malley estimated off the top of his head that about 1,200 spaces were used during weeks 3 and 4. What estimation method did he use? ____________

10. About how many parking spaces were used the first two weeks? ____________

11. How can you use compatible numbers to estimate the total parking spaces used for all five weeks? ____________

12. "What's the range of cars parking in the two highest weeks?" Mr. O'Malley wondered. What is the range? ____________

13. Last summer in the softball league, Andrea and Colleen hit a combined total of 13 home runs. Colleen hit 3 more than Andrea. Use "guess and check" to figure out the number of home runs Andrea hit. ____________

14. There are a total of 21 miles of bike path on the Old Plank Road. There are 5 more miles paved than unpaved. How many miles are paved and how many unpaved?

____

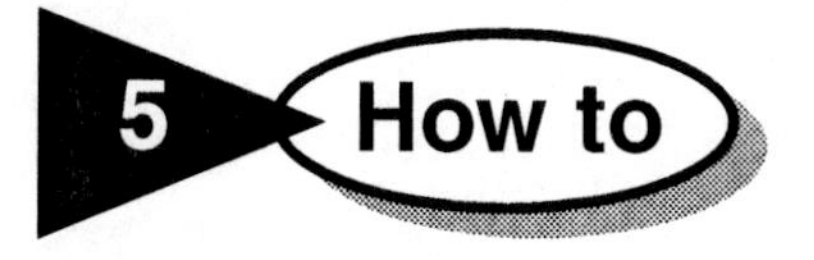

Recognize Extra Information in Word Problems

Facts to Know

Sometimes a problem has extra information that you do not need to solve the problem. But before you start these problems, keep in mind that you need to ask yourself these four important questions:

- *What does the problem ask you to find?*
- *What information is needed to solve the problem?*
- *How can you show the problem with numbers?*
- *What is your answer?*

Sample A

At the art fair, Libby bought a mug of root beer for $1, a veggie burger for $2, a hot fudge sundae for $2, and a piece of pottery for $5. How much did Libby spend on food?

First, focus on the information you need to answer the question being asked. Then identify the extra information that is not necessary for answering the question because it has no effect on the answer.

In the problem above, the question is about money spent on food. So the extra information is that Libby bought a piece of pottery for $5.

Now, you can solve the problem using only the information that's necessary.

$1 + $2 + $2 = $5

Libby spent $5 on food.

Sample B

Erica and her friends had a pizza party. They ordered 8 pizzas. $\frac{1}{2}$ of the pizzas were large combo pizzas, $\frac{1}{4}$ of the pizzas were medium specialty pizzas, and $\frac{1}{4}$ were medium pepperoni pizzas. They also ordered five 2-liter sodas for $1.50 each. How many medium pepperoni pizzas did Erica and her friends order?

First, focus on the information you need to answer the question being asked. Then identify the extra information that is not necessary for answering the question because it has no effect on the answer.

In the problem above, the question is about how many medium pepperoni pizzas were ordered. So the extra information is how many sodas and large combo pizzas, were ordered by Erica and her friends.

Now you can solve the problem using only the information that's necessary.

Erica and her friends ordered 2 medium pepperoni pizzas.

5 Practice •••••••••• Identifying Extra Information in Word Problems

Directions: Using the information on page 21, solve the problems below and on pages 23 and 24.

Russian rubles are interesting coins. They are sometimes smaller than ours. How many Russian rubles can you buy with $300.00 if 20 rubles are worth a dollar?

1. What does the problem ask you to find?

a. how many rubles is $300

b. how many dollars are 20 rubles

c. how much less are rubles worth than dollars

d. how many rubles can you buy with $300

2. What is the extra information in the problem?

e. Russian rubles are interesting coins

f. 20 rubles are worth a dollar

g. rubles are sometimes smaller than our coins

h. e and g

3. How can you show the problem with numbers?

i. $300 x 20 rubles/$1 =

j. $300 x $1 x 20 rubles =

k. $300 x $\frac{20}{100}$ =

l. $\frac{20}{300}$ x $1.00 =

4. What is your answer?

m. 6,000 rubles

n. 600 rubles

o. 3,000 rubles

p. 60,000 rubles

The train-station parking lot has space for 1,000 cars. $\frac{2}{5}$ of the spaces are for standardized cars. Many commuters arrived late for the train. On Tuesday, there were 200 standardized cars and some standard-size cars in the parking lot. The parking lot was $\frac{3}{4}$ full. How many standard-size cars were in the parking lot?

5. What does the problem ask you to find?

a. how many spaces are for standard-size cars

b. how many spaces were empty

c. how many standard-size cars were in the parking lot

d. how many compact cars could still squeeze in

6. What is the extra information in the problem?

e. the train station parking lot has space for 1,000 cars

f. $\frac{2}{5}$ of the spaces are for standardized cars

g. many commuters arrived late for the train

h. the parking lot was $\frac{3}{4}$ full

 © Teacher Created Resources, Inc.

Identifying Extra Information in Word Problems

7. How can you show the problem with numbers? ______________________________

Hint: *Keep in mind that the lot holds 1,000 cars, and it was $\frac{3}{4}$ full. How many total cars were there?*

8. What is your answer?

i. 750 cars
j. 550 standard-size cars
k. 600 standard-size cars
l. 1,750 cars

Julio runs $\frac{3}{10}$ mile in $1\frac{1}{2}$ minutes. If he keeps running at that rate on a day when the wind is blowing against him, how long will it take him to run one mile?

9. What does the problem ask you to find?

a. how much will the wind slow him down
b. how far does he have to run
c. how fast can he run
d. how long will it take him to run one mile

10. What is the extra information in the problem?

e. he runs $\frac{3}{10}$ mile in $1\frac{1}{2}$ minutes
f. the wind is blowing against him
g. he will keep running at that rate
h. he is going to run one mile

11. How can you show the problem with numbers? ______________________________

Hint: *There is a formula for figuring out problems like this one. First, figure out Julio's rate per $1\frac{1}{2}$ minutes: ($\frac{3}{10}$ mile) ÷ ($1\frac{1}{2}$ minutes) = rate per $1\frac{1}{2}$ minutes. (Remember to use the reciprocal for the second fraction and multiply). Once you get his rate, use this formula:*

t (time) = d (distance) ÷ r (rate)

12. What is your answer?

i. 10 minutes
j. 5 minutes
k. .05 minutes
l. 1 minute

A computer disk holds 720k of memory. The disks come 10 in a pack for $3.95. If three programs are on a disk and they use 27k, 34k, and 52k of memory, how much memory is left on the disk?

13. What does the problem ask you to find?

a. how much does each disk cost
b. how much memory is left on the disk
c. what is the total space being used on the disk
d. how much space is available on a disk

14. What is the extra information in the problem?

e. A computer disk can hold 720k of information.
f. Three programs are on a disk.
g. The three programs use 27k, 34k, and 52k of memory.
h. The disks come 10 in a pack for $3.95.

15. How can you show the problem with numbers?
    i. 27k + 34k + 52k = 113k; then 720k – 113k =
    j. $3.95 ÷ 10 = $.395 x 113k
    k. 113k x 3 =
    l. 3(27k + 34k + 52k) =

16. And what is your answer?
    m. 607k
    n. 339k
    o. 2,010k
    p. none of these

The Chang Toy Factory in China can produce 35 miniature toy cars each minute at a cost of 77 cents. Then, a package of 35 is put in a cardboard box that holds 350. What does it cost to produce 385 toy cars?

17. What does the problem ask you to find?
    a. how much does a box of 385 cars sell for
    b. what does it cost to produce 385 toy cars
    c. what is the cost of each toy car
    d. how much does a box of 350 cars cost

18. What is the extra information in the problem?
    e. a package of 35 is put in a cardboard box that holds 350
    f. 35 toy cars are produced each minute
    g. at a cost of 77 cents
    h. what does it cost to produce 385 toy cars

19. How can you show the problem with numbers?
    i. $.77 ÷ 35 = $0.022; then 385 cars x $0.022 =
    j. $.77 x 35 = $26.95; then $26.95 x 385 =
    k. $.77 x 35 = $26.95; then $26.95 ÷ 385 =
    l. 385 ÷ 35 =

20. What is your answer?
    m. $10,375.75
    n. $.07
    o. $8.47
    p. $.11

 © Teacher Created Resources, Inc.

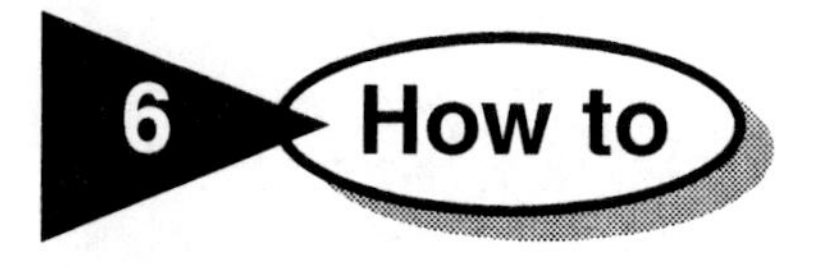

Solve for Fractions, Decimals, Percents, and Ratios

Facts to Know

The key to solving word problems involving fractions, decimals, percents, and ratios is understanding how the same amount can be shown each of the four ways:

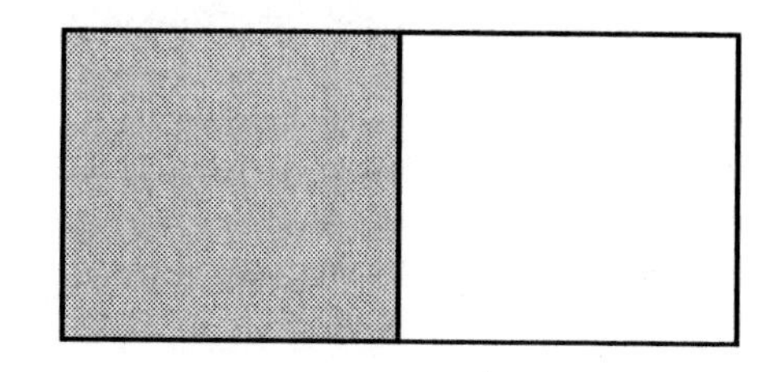

- $\frac{1}{2}$ of the bar is shaded.
- The amount of the shaded portion is .5.
- 50% of the bar is shaded.
- The ratio of the length of the bar to its shaded portion is 2:1.

You can hear how decimals are like fractions. Say a decimal out loud. It sounds like a fraction.

0.50 → Say "fifty hundredths."

$\frac{50}{100}$ → Say "fifty hundredths."

In the same way, percent means "per hundred." Hundredths or percents can be used for the same number.

$$\frac{50}{100} = 0.50 = 50\%$$

A ratio is used to compare two numbers. A ratio can be written in any one of three ways. If three out of five students in class are girls, this can be written as:

3 to 5 → 3:5 → $\frac{3}{5}$ → You read this ratio as "three to five."

Another way to look at percent is this: a percent is a ratio of some number to 100. Imagine a 10 x 10 square grid. If there were 40 shaded squares out of 100 total (a ratio of 40 to 100), you could say "40% are shaded."

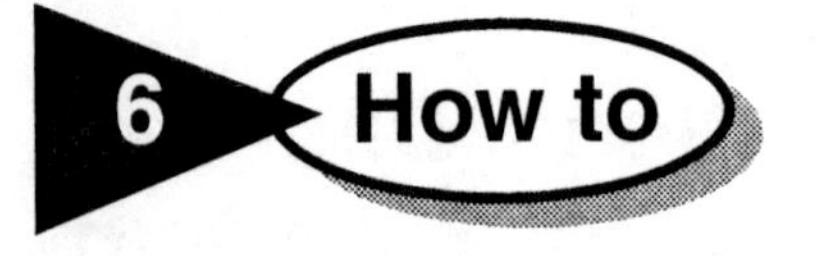

Solve for Fractions, Decimals, Percents, and Ratios

Facts to Know

Changing Fractions to Decimals

There are two ways to change fractions to decimals. The first is to rewrite the fraction to make its denominator a decimal equivalent in tenths, hundredths, or thousandths.

First way: Multiply the numerator and denominator of the fraction by the same number so the denominator comes out as a tenth, hundredth, or thousandth.

Sample A: Change $\frac{1}{2}$ to a decimal.

Step 1 → Multiply $\frac{1}{2}$ by $\frac{5}{5}$ (1) so the result is a denominator as a tenth.

Step 2 → Rewrite $\frac{5}{10}$ as a decimal: 0.5, which is the same amount (say, "five-tenths").

$$\frac{1}{2} \times \frac{5}{5} = \frac{5}{10}$$ (The denominator is in tenths.)

Sample B: Change $\frac{3}{4}$ to a decimal.

Step 1 → Multiply $\frac{3}{4}$ by $\frac{25}{25}$ (1) so the result is a denominator as a hundredth.

$$\frac{3}{4} \times \frac{25}{25} = \frac{75}{100}$$ (The denominator is in hundredths.)

Step 2 → Rewrite $\frac{3}{4}$ as a decimal: 0.75, which is the same amount (say, "seventy-five hundredths")

Second way: For fractions whose denominators are not equivalent to tenths, hundredths, or thousandths, divide the numerator by the denominator.

Sample C: Change $\frac{1}{3}$ to a decimal.

Step 1 → Add a decimal point after the numerator and add two zeros.

$$3\overline{)1.00}$$

Step 2 → Divide the numerator by the denominator. (In cases where the decimal repeats, put a bar over the number that repeats.)

Step 3 → Write the remainder as a fraction.

$$0.33\tfrac{1}{3} = 0.333$$

$$\begin{array}{r} 0.33 \\ 3\overline{)1.00} \\ -9\downarrow \\ \hline 10 \\ -9 \\ \hline 1 \end{array}$$

 © Teacher Created Resources, Inc.

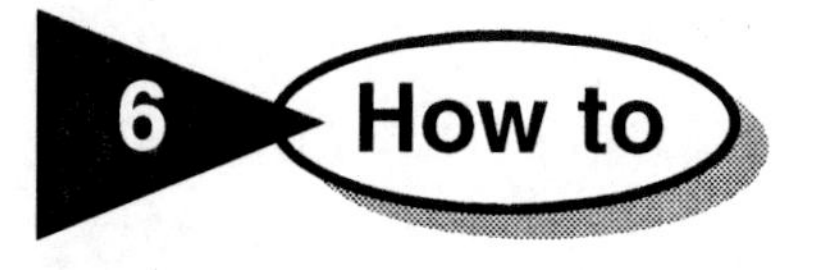

Solve for Fractions, Decimals, Percents, and Ratios

Facts to Know *(cont.)*

Changing Decimals to Percents

Changing a decimal to a percent requires that you change the decimal to hundredths first. You can do this in one of two ways.

First way: Change the decimal to an equivalent fraction.

Sample D: Change .7 to a percent.

Step 1 → Write the decimal as a fraction. $0.7 = \frac{7}{10}$

Step 2 → If necessary, change the fraction to an equivalent fraction with a denominator of 100. (Remember, percent means "per hundred.") $\frac{7}{10} \times \frac{10}{10} = \frac{70}{100}$

Step 3 → Change the fraction to a percent. $\frac{70}{100} = 70\%$

Second way: Move the decimal point two places to the right and include the percent sign. This is the same as multiplying the decimal by a hundred.

Sample E: Change .7 to a percent **.70 = 70%**

Changing Fractions to Percents

There are two ways to change fractions to percents. The first is to change the fraction to an equivalent fraction with a denominator of 100. The second, for fractions that cannot be changed to equivalent fractions with denominators of 100, is to change the fraction to a decimal and then from a decimal to a percent.

First way: Change the fraction to a percent by using an equivalent fraction.

Sample F: Change $\frac{2}{5}$ to a percent.

Step 1 → If the denominator of the fraction is a factor of 100, change the fraction to an equivalent fraction with a denominator of 100. $\frac{2}{5} \times \frac{20}{20} = \frac{40}{100}$

Step 2 → Change the new fraction to a percent. $\frac{40}{100} = 40\%$

Second way: Change the fraction to a percent using the decimal method.

Sample G: Change $\frac{4}{9}$ to a percent.

Step 1 → For fractions whose denominators are not factors of 100, divide the numerator by the denominator.

Step 2 → Add a decimal point and two zeros.

Step 3 → Divide. Write any remainder as a fraction.

Step 4 → Change the decimal to a percent.

$$\begin{array}{r} 0.44\frac{4}{9} \\ 9\overline{)4.00} \\ -36\downarrow \\ \hline 40 \\ -36 \\ \hline 4 \end{array} \quad = 44\tfrac{4}{9}\%$$

Solving Fractions, Decimals, Percents, and Ratios

Directions: Using the information on pages 25–27, solve the problems on this page.

1. Jan has 25 cookies and has invited 10 friends to share them with her. If everyone gets a fair share, how much does each person get? ____________

2. Eve, Colin, Toby, Bob, George, Brandon, Nick, Matt, Larry, Chris, and Madison went to the mall. Each person all spent $\frac{1}{5}$ of $25 that each had, and Bob in addition bought three people gum for $0.25 each. How much money did they spend in all? ____________

3. Marcy's dad is a car dealer. He paid $12,456.75 for a car. He wishes to make a profit of $2,300. How much should he sell it for? ____________

4. Ina earns $8.00 an hour bagging groceries at the supermarket. She worked 18.5 hours last week. How much money did she make last week? ____________

5. When the Panthers practice, 8 balls are used by 16 players. How many balls will 32 players need? ____________

6. The community playhouse was selling tickets. The ratio of adult tickets to student tickets was 3 to 5. If they sold 30 adult tickets, how many student tickets did they sell? ____________ If they sold 60 adult tickets, how many student tickets did they sell? ____________

7. This year 80 girls tried out for the cheerleading squad. After tryouts, the coach told the girls he could only accept 15% of the girls on Team A, while the rest of the girls could be on Team B. How many girls can be on Team B? ____________

8. Marco had 300 baseball cards. Marco told his friend Juan that he would give Marco 75% of his collection of 300 baseball cards. How many cards is Juan going to give to Marco? ____________

9. Ellen bought a sweater for $35.00. If the sweater was on sale for 30% off, what was the original price of the sweater that Ellen bought? ____________

10. Ramon bought 4 tickets for an upcoming music concert. He paid $130 for the tickets. If Ramon and his mother, father, and sister are going to the concert, how much is each ticket? ____________

 © Teacher Created Resources, Inc.

7 How to •••• Look for a Pattern in Word Problems

Facts to Know

Some problems can be solved by recognizing a pattern. Making a table can help you.

Sample A

David arranged loaves of bread on 6 shelves in the bakery. He put 1 loaf on the top shelf, 3 loaves on the second shelf, and 5 loaves on the third shelf. If he continues this pattern, how many loaves will he put on the 6th shelf?

If you make a table, you'll see a pattern.

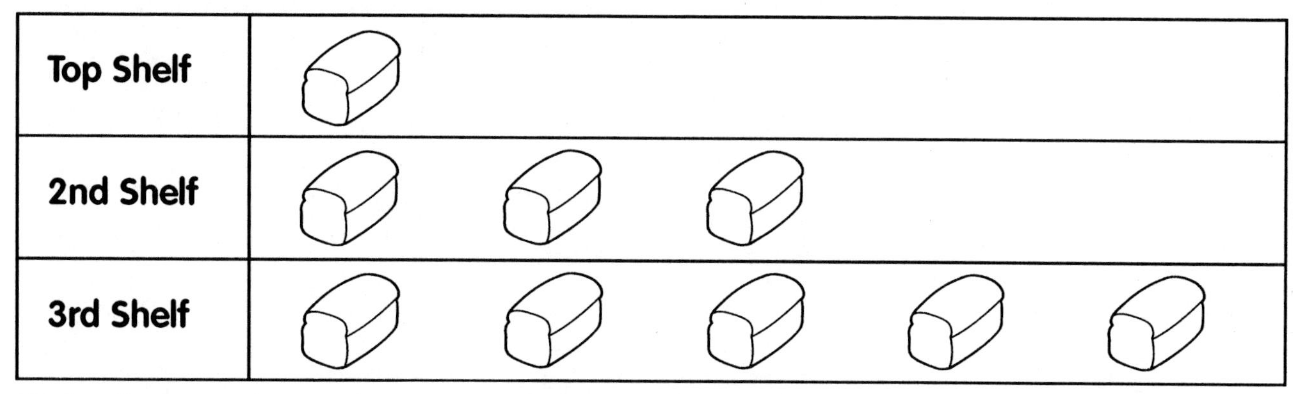

Notice there are 2 more loaves on each shelf. If you complete the pattern, you'll know how many loaves are on the 6th shelf. (11 loaves)

Sample B

Monday through Thursday, Teresa exercises for 30 minutes after coming home from work. On the weekends, she goes swimming for 1 hour on Saturday. Teresa does not exercise on Friday and Sunday. At the end of 2 weeks, how much time will she have spent exercising?

If you make a table or chart, you'll see the pattern and be able to calculate how much time Teresa will have exercised in 2 weeks. (6 hours)

Week 1

Days of the Week	Monday	Tuesday	Wednesday	Thursday	Friday	Saturday	Sunday
Exercise Time	30 minutes	30 minutes	30 minutes	30 minutes	no exercise	1 hour	no exercise

Week 2

Days of the Week	Monday	Tuesday	Wednesday	Thursday	Friday	Saturday	Sunday
Exercise Time	30 minutes	30 minutes	30 minutes	30 minutes	no exercise	1 hour	no exercise

7 Practice • • • Solving Word Problems with Patterns

Directions: Using the information on page 29, solve the problems on this page.

1. David is trying to crack a mysterious code. He's made a chart, but there are missing numbers. Look at the chart and fill in the numbers.

   He knows that the key is to find a pattern. (*Hint:* Look at the columns.)

Code Box

4	5	9	___	___	___	16	___	7
2	2	4	___	5	7	___	1	___
2	3	5	6	___	8	___	2	4
4	6	20	42	25	___	63	2	12

2. An ice-cream stand has nine different flavors. A group of children come to the stand and each buys a double-scoop cone with two flavors of ice cream. If none of the children choose the same combination of flavors and every different combination of flavors is chosen, how many children are there? ________

Ice Cream List

1 Vanilla	4 Marble Mocha	7 Coffee
2 Butter Pecan	5 Raspberry	8 Chocolate Mint
3 Chocolate	6 Strawberry	9 Cherry Vanilla

Hint: *The number of children = number of different combinations of two different flavors. Continue this pattern:*

1,2	2,3	3,4	4,5	5,6	6,7	7,8	8,9
1,3	2,4	__,__	4,6	__,__	__,__	__,__	
1,4	__,__	__,__	__,__	5,8	6,9		
1,5	__,__	__,__	__,__	5,9			
1,6	2,7	__,__	4,9				
__,__	__,__	__,__					
__,__	__,__						
__,__							

3. a. If you saved $2.00 on January 1, $4.00 on February 1, $6.00 on March 1, $8.00 on April 1, and so on, how much money would you save in one year? __________

   b. If you saved $2.00 on January 1, $4.00 on February 1, $8.00 on March 1, $16.00 on April 1, and so on. How much money would you save in one year? __________

Hint: *Notice the patterns of the amounts in the two questions.*

• • • Solving Word Problems with Patterns

4. Rob wanted an allowance. His father gave him a choice of getting it on a weekly or on a daily basis. He said he would either pay him $1.25 a week or pay him in the following manner for a week: On Monday he would give him $0.01; on Tuesday $0.02; on Wednesday $0.04; and on through Sunday. What would you tell Rob to do so he can get more allowance?

Hint: *Continue the pattern of doubling the number of cents through Sunday.*

____

5. Suppose today is Tuesday. What day of the week is it 100 days from now?

Hint: *Start by dividing 100 by 7 because every seventh day is a Tuesday.*

____

6. Mr. Grimly rents apartments. He carefully keeps track of his building's daily use of kilowatt hours of electricity as he rents more and more apartments. Complete his table:

Renters	1	2	3	4	5	6	7	8	9	10
Kilowatt hours	2	5	7	10	12					

7. Art Ringwald's Auto World sent letters to 5,000 residents offering them the chance to win a free car. Art received 200 replies. A month later, he sent 6,000 letters and received 240 replies. If the pattern continues, how many replies can the company expect to receive if it sends 8,000 notices? ________

Hint: *Figure the amount for 7,000 first.*

8. Bill Phelps is a gas meter reader. It takes him 10 minutes to read 30 meters. He can read 60 meters in 20 minutes, and 90 meters in 30 minutes. If the pattern continues, how long does it take him to read 150 meters? ________

Hint: *The key is "It takes him 10 minutes to read 30 meters."*

9. The women who belong to the library book club met on May 17, June 14, and July 12. If this pattern continues, when is their next meeting? ________

Hint: *Use a calendar.*

10. Leonardo Fibonacci, an Italian mathematician who lived from about 1180 to 1250, found a pattern in numbers. Mathematicians are still discovering that this pattern can be seen in nature in the way things grow. Here is the pattern:

0, 1, 1, 2, 3, 5, 8, 13, 21, 34, 55, 89, 144, 233, ___ ___ ___, ___ ___ ___, ___ ___ ___

Do you recognize the pattern? What goes in the blanks?

Hint: *2 + 3 = 5*

11. As you come into the Museum of Technology, you notice a rocket on a platform that turns. The rocket always points north at 9 A.M.; east at 9:15 A.M.; south at 9:30 A.M.; west at 9:45 A.M.; and north again at 10 A.M. Which direction will it be pointing at 6:15 P.M., more than 9 hours later? __________

12. Can you solve this magic square?

Put the remaining numbers from 0 to 15 in the 16 small squares. The sum of the four numbers in each row, column, and two diagonals must be 30.

15			12
	10	9	
			11
3			0

13. Five friends exchange valentines on Valentine's Day. How many valentines are exchanged?

Hint: *Start with a smaller number as an experiment. What if there were only one person? Then no valentines exchanged—zero. What if there were only two friends instead of five? Then there would be 2 valentines exchanged. Three friends—there would be 6 exchanged. Four friends—there would be 12.*

What's the pattern? 0, 2, 6, 12,...? ____________________

14. What is the syllable pattern of this limerick, and what is the rhyme pattern? __________

____

There was an Old Man with a nose,
Who said, "If you choose to suppose,
That my nose is too long,
You are certainly wrong!"
That remarkable Man with a nose.

15. Cans of tuna are arranged in a display that has 4 rows. Each row has one more can than the row above it. If the last row has 10 cans, how many cans are in the display?

____

 © Teacher Created Resources, Inc.

8 How to • • • • Solve Measurement Word Problems

Facts to Know

Solving most measurement problems requires that you know your basic operations—addition, subtraction, division, and multiplication. Often you must be comfortable with fractions, decimals, percents, and ratios too. You can go back to Unit 6 for a review if you need to.

Second, you should have measurement tables you can depend on or have simple facts like these memorized:

Length	Liquid Volume	Weight
Customary to Metric	**Customary to Metric**	**Customary to Metric**
1 in. = 2.54 cm	1 cup = 240 mL	1 oz. = 28.4 g
1 ft. = 30 cm	1 pint = 0.47 L	1 lb. = 0.45 kg
1 yard = 0.91 m	1 quart = 0.95 L	**Customary**
1 mile = 1.6 km	1 gallon = 3.79 L	1 lb. = 16 oz.
Customary	**Customary**	1 ton = 2,000 lbs.
1 ft. = 12 in.	1 teaspoon = 1/6 fl. oz.	
1 yard = 3 ft.	1 tablespoon = 3 teaspoons = 1/2 fl. oz.	
1 mile = 5,280 ft.	1 cup = 8 fl. oz.	
1 mile = 1,760 yards	1 pint = 2 cups	
	1 quart = 2 pints	
	1 gallon = 128 fl. oz.	
	1 gallon = 4 quarts	

And third, you must know basic formulas:

Finding Perimeter		Finding Area	
rectangle or parallelogram	**$P = 2l + 2w$**	**rectangle**	**$A = lw$**
square	**$P = 4s$**	**square**	**$A = s^2$**
circle	**$C = \pi d$ or $C = 2\pi r$**	**circle**	**$A = \pi r^2$**

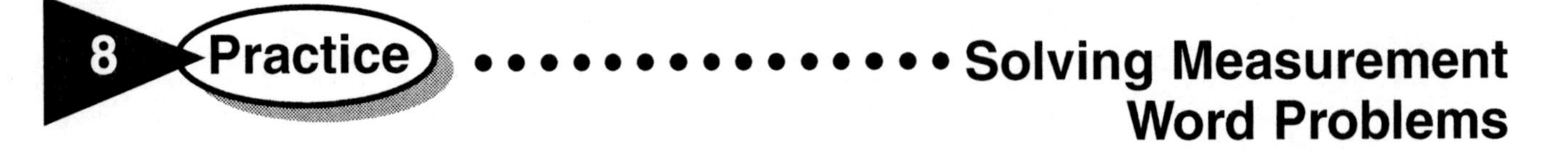

Solving Measurement Word Problems

Directions: Using the information on page 33, solve the problems below and on page 35.

1. The students in art are drawing plans of their ideal school. They're trying to be as accurate as possible, so they wrote down their questions. Being a math whiz, you have volunteered to figure the answers.
   a. The volleyball net is 1 m wide and 9.50 m long. What is the perimeter of the net? __________ What is the area of the net? __________
   b. The service area in volleyball is 3 m long and 3 m wide. What is the perimeter of the service? __________ What is the area of the service area? __________
   c. The volleyball court is 18 m long and 9 m wide. It is divided into two halves. What is the perimeter of the court? __________ What is the area of each side? __________
   d. The art students are thinking about putting a running track around the perimeter of the volleyball court. If someone ran 3 times around, how far would that be? __________

2. Kyle and Luke were in charge of making punch for a party in their class. They collected the money from their classmates and then got the recipe from Kyle's mom. It said:

Party Punch

6-ounce can frozen lemonade
4 cups orange juice
2 cups white grape juice
2 cups carbonated water
4 pints ginger ale

Kyle shook his head and said, "We can't buy these things in these amounts." "You're right," said Luke. "Let's rewrite the recipe."

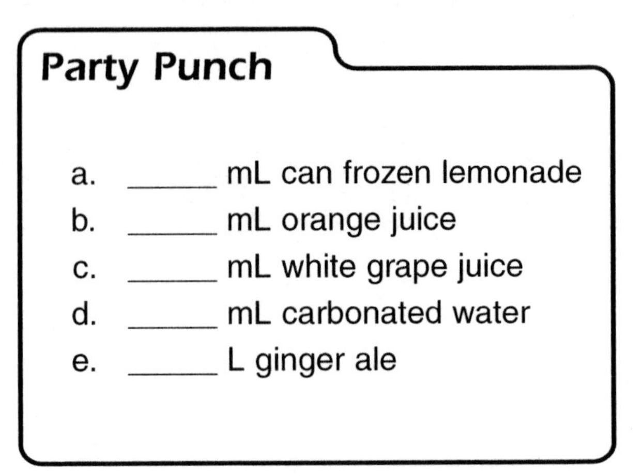

3. Spencer has agreed to do a project for his father in exchange for a new snowboard this winter. Spencer needs to paint the garden shed in his back yard. His father needs to buy the paint for the shed and has asked Spencer to measure the size of each wall to determine the amount of paint he should purchase.
   a. After measuring the walls, Spencer has determined that each wall is 7 feet high and 12 feet long. What is the area of each wall? __________
   b. What is the total area of the walls around the shed? __________
   c. If a quart of paint covers 100 square feet, how many quarts of paint must Spencer's father purchase? __________

4. Spencer's dad gets to the hardware store and sees a sign that advertises a gallon of the paint he wants to use is on sale for $13.50. He looks at the price for a quart of the paint, and it sells for $3.25. Should Spencer's father buy the gallon or the quarts? __________

 © Teacher Created Resources, Inc.

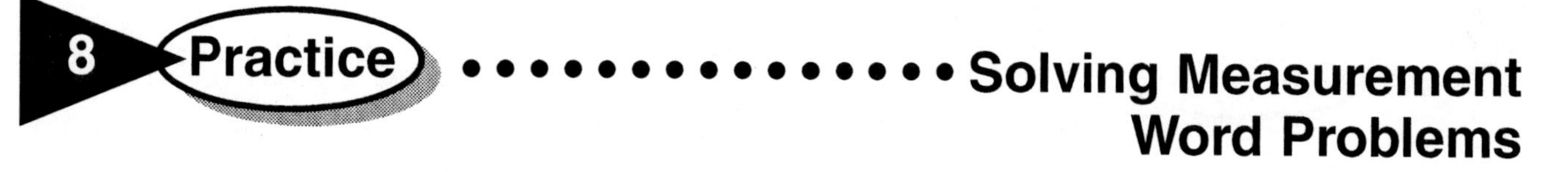

5. Tom's parents measure Tom every fall. Last year his height was 63 inches. This year his height is 66 inches. Two years ago his height was 60 inches.

   a. How many inches has he grown in three years? ________________

   b. What is Tom's current height in feet and inches? ________________

6. Sam's height is 66 inches. Paula is 4 inches shorter than Sam and 2 inches taller than Mary. Tom is 2 inches shorter than Mary.

   a. Arrange the children from the shortest to the tallest. ________________

   b. What is the height of the each child in centimeters?
   Sam ________ Paula ________ Mary ________ Tom ________

7. Kristin is baking a cake. She needs 2 cups of flour. How many milliliters is 2 cups of flour? ________

8. Mrs. Norris is canning tomatoes. She must put $\frac{1}{2}$ teaspoon of salt in a pint of tomatoes. How much salt would she put in a quart of tomatoes? ________

9. Bill is remodeling his house. He needs four boards that measure 10.8 m each.

   a. How many feet is each board? ________

   b. Change the answer to inches. ________

10. Jessica is making a dress. She needs three yards of cloth. How many inches of cloth will she need? ________

11. Mr. O'Leary is remodeling his kitchen. He needs four boxes of tile. If one box of tile will cover 20 feet of floor, how much will four boxes of tile cover? ________

12. Margie uses 7.62 cm of ribbon to make a hair bow. If she wants to make five hair bows, how many inches of ribbon will she need? ________

13. Heather has a pet that weighs 80 ounces. How many pounds is that? ________

14. Mrs. Norris bought a ham that weighed 3.15 kg. How many pounds is that? ________

15. An elephant weighs 4,000 pounds. How many tons is that? ________

16. Baby Jane drank a 16-ounce glass of orange juice. How many cups would that be? ________

17. William drank a 1.90 L glass of orange juice. How many pints of orange juice would that be? ________

18. Mrs. Norris will can green beans this summer. She wants to can 8 quarts of green beans at one time, but she only has pint jars. How many pint jars would she need? ________

19. A bridge can hold only 4 tons of weight. Can a truck that weighs 2,300 pounds and a car weighing 2,300 pounds be on the bridge at the same time? ________

20. Tom and Gabriel are training for the track team. Tom runs 3.12 miles each morning. Gabriel runs about 4.4 km. Who runs the longer distance? ________

Use Basic Operations in Word Problems

Facts to Know

All the problems in this unit can be solved using basic operations of subtracting, adding, multiplying or dividing fractions, decimals, and percents. Use them as a review of your fundamental skills.

Sample A

Mrs. King bought a dozen muffins for the students in her classroom. If she bought, $\frac{1}{2}$ of a dozen chocolate chip, $\frac{1}{4}$ of a dozen apple cinnamon, and $\frac{1}{4}$ dozen banana nut, how many of each muffin did she buy?

Hint: *Remember that 1 dozen muffins = 12 muffins*

First, calculate what fraction of the 1 dozen muffins is of what variety.

$\frac{1}{2}$ dozen chocolate chip = 6 chocolate chip muffins

$\frac{1}{4}$ dozen apple cinnamon = 3 apple cinnamon muffins

$\frac{1}{4}$ dozen banana nut = 3 banana nut muffins

Then, add the different types of muffins and see if they add up to a dozen muffins.

6 chocolate chip + 3 apple cinnamon + 3 banana nut = 12 muffins

Sample B

Kenny and Kendra each received $10 to spend at the movies. Kenny bought his ticket for $4.50 and then bought a small soda for $2.00 and popcorn for $2.50. How much money did Kenny spend, and did he have any money left? Kendra spent $4.50 for her ticket and then paid $1.75 for red licorice sticks and $2.00 for a small soda. How much money did Kendra spend, and did she have any money left?

Kenny		Kendra	
First, add up all the money that Kenny spent at the movie theater.	Next, subtract the total amount that Kenny spent from the $10 that he was given.	Now, add up all the money that Kendra spent at the movie theater.	Next, subtract the total amount that Kendra spent from the $10 that she was given.
$4.50 *ticket* **$2.00** *small soda* **+ $2.50** *popcorn* **$9.00**	**$10.00** **– $9.00** **$1.00**	**$4.50** *ticket* **$1.75** *red licorice* **$2.00** *small soda* **$8.25**	**$10.00** **– $8.25** **$1.75**
So Kenny spent $9.00 at the theater and had $1.00 left.		So Kendra spent $8.25 at the theater and had $1.75 left.	

 © Teacher Created Resources, Inc.

9 Practice •••••••••••••••• Word Problems Using Basic Operations

Directions: Using the information on page 36 and the previous units as reference, solve the problems on this page. (*Suggestion:* Challenge yourself and see how quickly you can complete them. Can you solve all 30 problems in an hour and a half?)

1. Tiffany's pan of fudge had 12 pieces. She sold $\frac{1}{3}$ of the fudge. How many pieces did she sell? ________
2. Andrew needed 3 quarts of punch for the bake sale. He had $\frac{3}{4}$ quart in one container, $\frac{1}{2}$ quart in another container, and $1\frac{1}{4}$ quart in another container. How much punch did he have? ________ Did he have enough punch for the bake sale? ________
3. How many dollars do you have if you have 6 quarters, 4 nickels, and 3 dimes? ________
4. The local store carries two kinds of veggie hot dogs:

Bark 'n' Bite Hot Dogs: 8 hot dogs for $3.20
Good Dog Hot Dogs: 6 hot dogs for $3.00

   a. How much does one Bark 'n' Bite hot dog cost? ________

   b. How much does one Good Dog hot dog cost? ________
5. The town band purchased a bass drum for $236.95, a trumpet for $165.39, and a saxophone for $207.10. What was the total cost of the instruments? ________
6. The fourth grade raised $67.23 for the play costumes; the fifth grade raised $87.23; the sixth grade raised $108.45; and the seventh grade raised $154.39. What was the total amount of their contribution? ________
7. Gabriel sold cookie boxes to raise money for his summer camp trip. He sold 8 boxes at $3.49 per box, 6 boxes at $4.49 per box, and 12 boxes at $2.98 per box. What was the total of his sales? ________
8. A bag of tortilla chips costs $3.49, and a jar of hot salsa costs $1.79. How much will 4 bags of chips and 3 jars of salsa cost? ________
9. Luke ordered 6 paperback books and 3 animal posters from a catalog. Each book cost $4.95. The posters cost $8.95 each. How much did he spend in all? ________
10. Jason bought 6 packs of baseball cards and paid $7.56. If each package cost the same amount, what was the cost of each package of cards? ________
11. If you buy an 18-ounce bottle of hot sauce, the cost is 68 cents. How much does the hot sauce cost per ounce? (Round to nearest hundredth.) ________
12. At a school luncheon, each pupil was served $\frac{1}{2}$ of a grapefruit. Thirty-two pupils were there. How many grapefruits were needed? ________
13. If 5 boys share a cantaloupe equally, is each boy's share more than $\frac{1}{4}$ of a cantaloupe? ________

Word Problems Using Basic Operations

14. Here's the lunch menu.

Lunch Menu

GIANT peanut butter and jelly sandwich	$2.50
Veggie Burger	$3.25
French Fries	$2.25
Salad	$2.75
Fruit Shake	$2.50
Spaghetti	$3.75

Paul had a veggie burger and a salad. Todd had a fruit shake, spaghetti, and a salad. Eli had two peanut butter and jelly sandwiches.
How much did each person spend? Paul ________ Todd ________ Eli ________
What was the total bill? ________

Lunch tickets are $8.00 (good for 5 lunches)

Milk tickets are $1.50 (good for 5 milks or juices)

15. Heather brings her bottled water from home, but she buys lunch. What will she pay for 10 lunches? ________ What will she pay for 20 lunches? ________

16. Mrs. Ochoa's fifth-grade class of 30 voted on their favorite season. If 40% voted for summer, 50% voted for winter, and 10% voted for spring, how many people voted for each season? ________________________________

17. Rita saves $2,500 each year for her retirement. That amount currently represents 8% of her total annual income. What is her annual income? ________

18. The Weather Bureau reported that the total rainfall for the first 7 months in Chicago was 30.93 inches. In August 1.02 inches, 2 inches, 1.6 inches, and 0.4 inch of rain fell on four days. What was the total rainfall at the end of the first 8 months? ________

19. If Jack and Chip get 24 tries at the carnival ring toss for $4, how many can they get for $1? ________

20. A grocery store has a sale on bananas. If you buy six bananas, you get the sale price. If the grocer has 489 bananas, how many bunches of six can he sell at his sale price? ________ In this case how many can be sold at the regular price? ________

21. Darcy worked 40 hours and earned $240. How much did she earn per hour? ________

22. Bruce had 280 pounds of big bolts. He put the same amount into each of 8 boxes. How much will the bolts weigh in each box? ________

 © Teacher Created Resources, Inc.

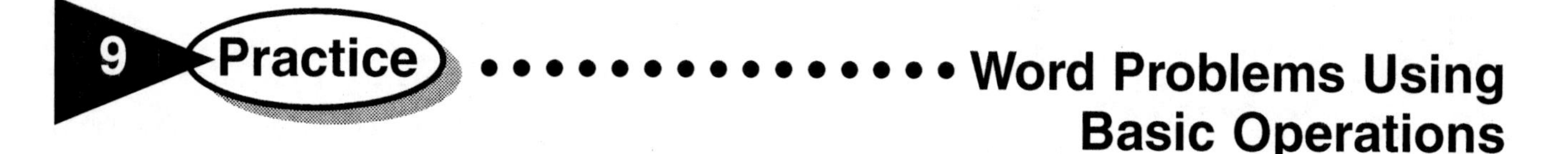

23. LaTonya worked 6 hours each on Monday, Wednesday, and Friday; she worked 10 hours each on Tuesday and Thursday. How many hours did she work altogether? ________ If she earns $7 an hour, how much money did she earn? ________

24. Which expression shows the total cost of 4 items at $7 each and 5 items at $6 each? _______ What is the total cost? _______

a. (4 + 5) x (6 + 7)
b. (4 x $7) + (5 x $6)
c. (7 x 5) – (6 x 4)
d. (4 + 7) ÷ (5 + 6)

25. Which expression shows the total weight of two crates that weigh 25 pounds each, four crates that weigh 40 pounds each, and five crates that each weigh 30 pounds. _______ What is the total weight? _______

a. 25 + 40 + 30
b. (2 + 4 + 5) x (25 + 40 + 30)
c. (25 x 4) + (40 x 30)
d. (2 x 25) + (4 x 40) + (5 x 30)

26. A clock is set correctly at 1:00 P.M. It loses 3 minutes every hour. What will the clock read when the correct time is 10:00 P.M.? _______

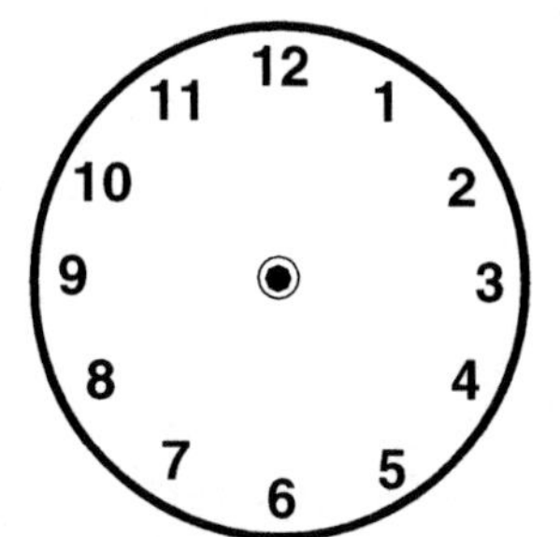

27. Four boys work together painting houses for the summer. For each house they paint they get $256.00. If the boys work for 4 months of summer and their expenses are $152.00 per month, how many houses must they paint for each of them to have one thousand dollars at the end of the summer? _______

28. The peel of a banana weighs about $\frac{1}{8}$ of the total weight of the banana. This is a little heavier than the peel of most fruit. If you buy 3 kg of bananas in a wood basket at $0.60 per kg, about how much are you paying for the banana peel? _______ How much for the banana itself? (Round to the nearest cent.) _______

29. James bought a video game for $29.95. He bought a computer CD-ROM game for $19.95. Both games were on sale for 25% off the ticketed price. How much did James spend to buy the video game and CD-ROM? _______ How much did he save? _______

30. Laurel and Joey went shopping for a birthday gift for their parents. They decided to buy a picture frame that costs $22.50. Laurel paid for 60% of the gift, and Joey paid for 40% of the gift. How much did each person pay for the gift? _______

Use Data from Graphs to Solve Word Problems

Sometimes word problems require you to read the data from graphs. Graphs usually do one of three things:

- Graphs can show the same kind of data at different times or places.
- Graphs can show the different kinds of data that make up 100% of a group.

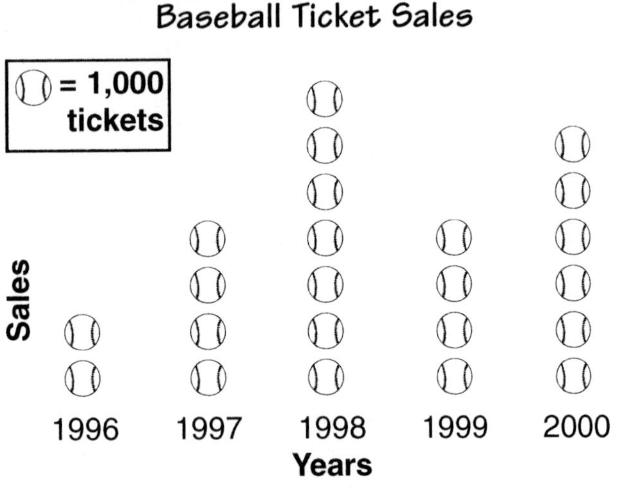

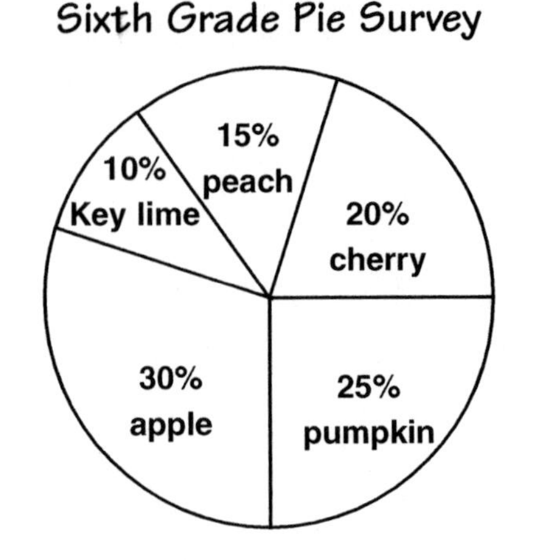

- Graphs can show different sets of data at the same time or place.

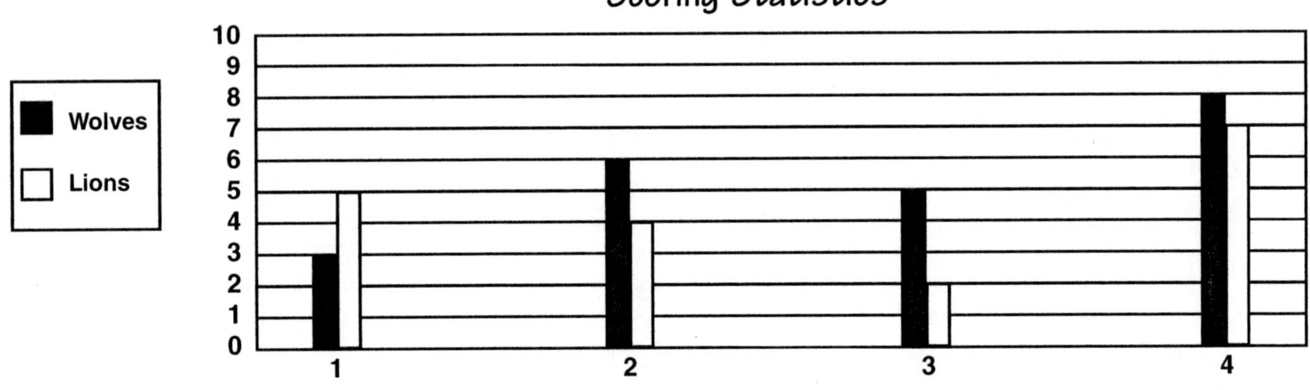

When a word problem asks you about information taken from a graph, think of the graph as words turned into a picture. If you have trouble understanding the graph, imagine explaining it to someone else. Turn the picture back into words.

Directions: Use the bar graph to answer each question.

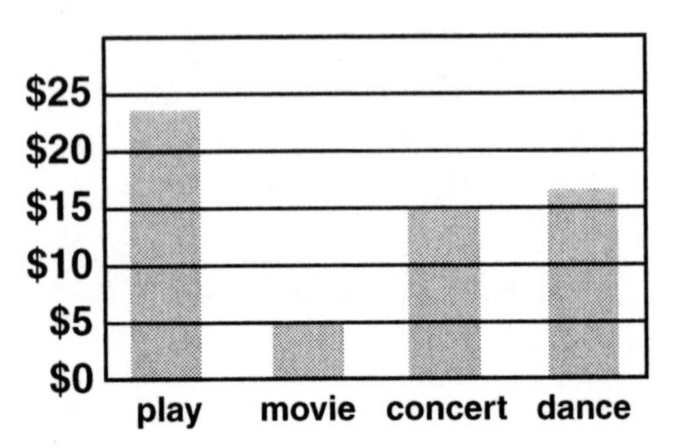

1. About how much does it cost to see a play? ________
2. Which activity is the most expensive? ________
3. Which activity is the least expensive? ________
4. Which activity costs less, a concert or a dance? ________
5. About how much more does it cost to go to a dance than to a concert? ________
6. If you saw a play, a movie, a concert, and a dance in one month, about how much money would you spend? ________

 © Teacher Created Resources, Inc.

Use Data from Graphs to Solve Word Problems

Directions: Use the bar graph to answer each question.

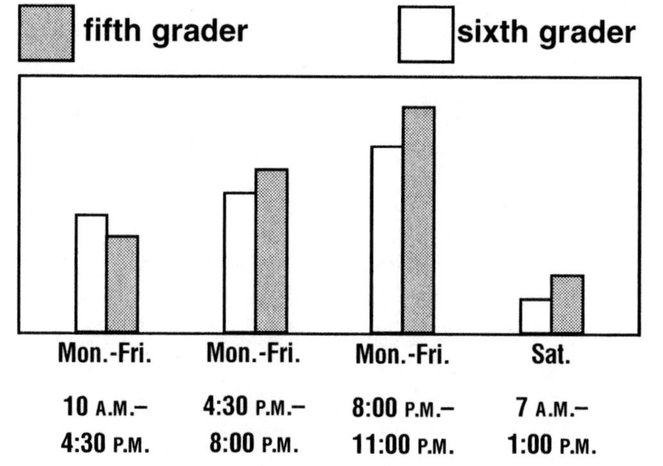

7. Do more fifth graders or sixth graders watch television on Saturday from 7 A.M. to 1 P.M.? _______
8. During which time period do fifth and sixth graders watch the greatest amount of television? _______
9. During which time period do fifth and sixth graders watch the least amount of television? _______

Directions: Use the pictograph below to answer the following questions.

This shows the number of drinks served in one day.

Grissom Cafeteria Drinks

[glass] = 100 glasses [half glass] = 50 glasses

Drink	Number of Glasses
white milk	[glass] [glass] [glass] [glass] [glass]
chocolate milk	[glass] [glass] [half glass]
orange juice	[glass] [glass]
apple juice	[glass] [half glass]

10. How many glasses of white milk did the cafeteria serve? _______
11. How many glasses of orange and apple juice were served? _______
12. How many more glasses of orange juice than apple juice were served? _______
13. How many glasses of drinks were served in one day? _______

Directions: Use the pie chart below to answer the following questions.

Animals in the Local Neighborhood

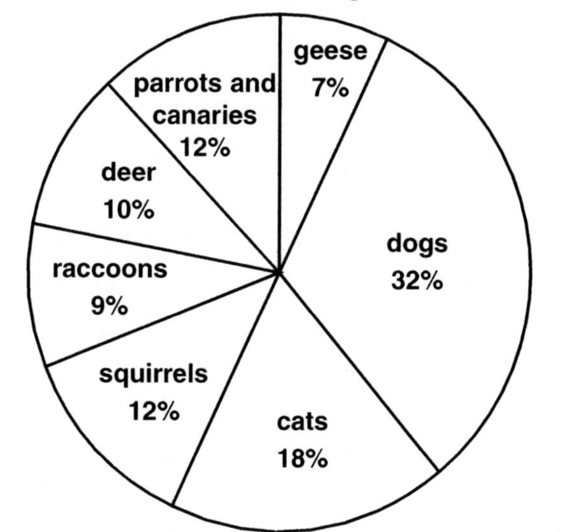

14. What percent of animals have wings? _______
15. What percent are house pets? _______
16. What percent have four legs? _______
17. What are the two most common wild animals in the neighborhood? _______

____

18. If you add the squirrels, the deer, and the different types of birds together, are there more or fewer of them than dogs? _______

Challenging Word Problems

Directions: Use some of the different methods you've learned to solve word problems in tackling these brain teasers.

Frog Race

Frog 1 and frog 2 have a race. Frog 1 makes a jump of 80 centimeters once every 5 seconds. Frog 2 makes a jump of 15 centimeters every 1 second. The rules of the race state that the frogs must cross a line 5 meters away and then return to the starting point. Which frog wins the race? _______

Bad Dogs!

Three neighborhood dogs barked all last night. Lolly, Patches, and Lady began barking together at 11:00 P.M. Then Lolly barked every 5 minutes, Patches barked every 8 minutes, and Lady barked every 12 minutes. Later that night, Mrs. Mikes awakened when all three dogs barked again together. What time did Mrs. Mikes wake up? _______

Free Dinner

At the Heartland Cafe, you get a free dinner after every 8 dinners you buy. If you ate there 45 times last year, how many of those dinners were free? _______

Race to Rescue

A child in a mountain village has fallen ill. Benjamin, his brother Joshua, and his sister Hannah must get their father, the village doctor, who is gathering herbs on the other side of the mountain. To make sure they get him as quickly as possible, they decide to split up.

> Joshua will ride his horse around the mountain's base.
> Benjamin will travel by river raft.
> Hannah will climb the steep cliff trail.

- The raft can travel at 22 miles an hour along the 40 miles of the river, but there are 3 places where Benjamin, at each place, will lose 0.4 hours by having to carry the raft past waterfalls.
- Joshua's horse can travel 15 miles per hour on the flatter part of the 32-mile trail but only 8 miles per hour on the steep part, which is 30% of the whole trail.
- Hannah's road up and down the cliffs is the shortest, only 14 miles, but her average rate is only 5 miles an hour, and she must take a 10-minute rest at the top of the trail.

Provided Benjamin does not hit a rock, Joshua is not attacked by wild animals, and Hannah is not bitten by a snake, who will reach their father first? (Round all decimals to tenths.) _______

 © Teacher Created Resources, Inc.

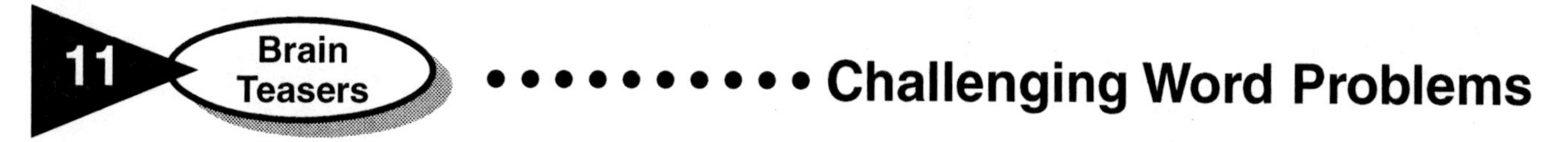

Challenging Word Problems

Clever Math Teachers

Math teachers just love playing math games. At Median Middle School, for example, the math teachers put signs on their doors to say whether they are at school or not. What they do is each post a true or untrue number sentence on the door. The teachers who are at school post problems with true answers. Here is what they posted last Tuesday.

Mr. Perry Meter:	4 x 12 = 12 + 12 + 12 + 12 + 12
Mr. Ric Tangle:	32,768 x 12,597 = 12,597 x 32,768
Ms. Py R. Square:	50 x 32 > 1,000
Mr. Sol Ution:	1/4 + 1/4 = 1/8
Ms. Dee Nominator:	572 x 43,176 = 572 x 43,196
Mr. Cal Culator:	33 + z = 107; z = 64

Who is in school? ______________________________

____

____

Who is not in school? ______________________________

____

____

At the Corner Store

Dave went into a corner store. He purchased four items.

"That will be $7.11," said the cashier.

"Wow! What a coincidence," Dave said. "How did you get $7.11?"

"Oh, I just multiplied the four items."

"What?! You're supposed to add the prices of the items, not multiply them."

"Makes no difference," said the cashier. "Comes out the same."

What were the prices of the four items?

Hint: *Three are under $2.00.*

Time Activity

Think how the day can be broken up into 24 hours. The time spent sleeping, eating, going to school, etc., can be expressed as fractional parts of the day. In this activity, 24 will be used as the denominator in all of the fractions. If you sleep 8 hours, then the fractional part of the day spent sleeping is 8/24. Use hours, not minutes. Show how you spend your 24-hour day as a chart. Make a fraction for each activity category in the day. You should total 24/24.

Bare Feet

There are 12 people in a room. 6 people are wearing socks, 4 people are wearing shoes, and 3 people are wearing both. How many people are in bare feet? ____________________

Two Trains Running (Everyone's Favorite)

A freight train leaves a station at 4:00 P.M. traveling at 30 kilometers per hour. A passenger train leaves 1 hour later, traveling at 50 kilometers per hour. At what time will the passenger train overtake the freight train?____________________

Hint: *Look at the problem as "starting" when both trains have started moving.*

Sheep or Kids?

This problem has more than one answer. Long ago, villagers were building a bridge. While working under the bridge, Rodney could see only the legs of those walking by. He counted 10 legs in one group. What combination of sheep and children could have been in that group?

____

Hint: *Guess and check different combinations.*

The Airplane and the Square

An airplane flies around a square which has sides 100 miles long. It takes the first side at 100 mph, the second side at 200 mph, the third side at 300 mph, and the fourth side at 400 mph.

What is the average speed of the plane in its flight around the square? ________

Hint: *This is another time/distance/rate problem. You need to find how long it took the airplane to travel each side for a total travel time.*

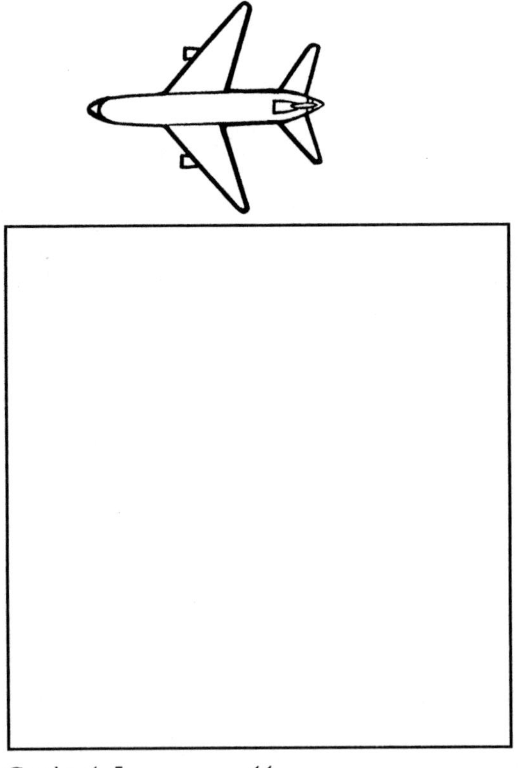

 © Teacher Created Resources, Inc.

Create a Word Problem Book on a Computer

Directions: Using a drawing program such as *Kid Pix*, follow the directions below to create a word problem book. A sample word problem book is provided on this page.

1. Using the Storyboarding Sheet on page 46, brainstorm about what types of problems and illustrations you want to create.
2. Create a cover page for your book. Use any of the stamps and drawing tools to illustrate your cover. Be sure to give your book a title and write your name on the cover.
3. Create as many problems as you want and use any stamps and drawing tools to illustrate your problems.
4. Save your work as you create each page. Print out your completed book.

Sample Word Problem Book

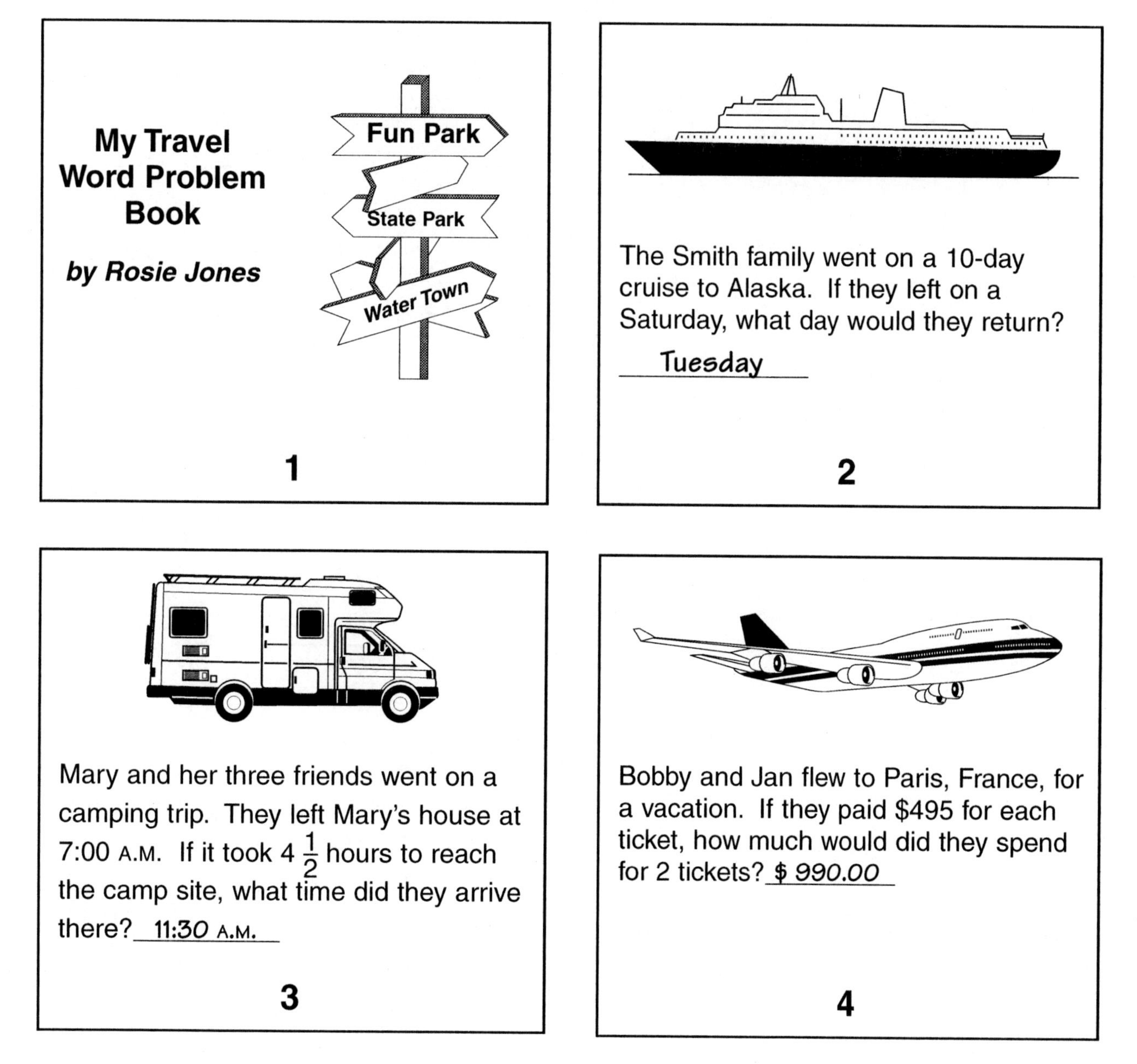

Create a Word Problem Book on a Computer

Storyboarding Sheet

 © Teacher Created Resources, Inc.

Answer Key

Pages 7 and 8

1. Step #1: c
   Step #2: f
   Step #3: i
   Step #4: m
2. Step #1: a
   Step #2: e
   Step #3: j
   Step #4: o
3. Step #1: c
   Step #2: g
   Step #3: j
   Step #4: n

Pages 10–12

1. c
2. (given)
3. h
4. j
   1,753 (2nd year)
   – 152 (less 3rd year)
   1,601 (3rd year total)

   1,572
   1,753
   + 1,601
   4,926
5. d
6. g
7. 110–95
   130–95
   116–95
8. j
   110 – 95 = 15 cookies leftover
   130 – 95 = 35 fudge leftover
   116 – 95 = 21 peanut butter squares left over
9. d
10. g
11. (given)
12. j
    Each day the grasshopper goes 1/8 m until the day when the grasshopper is at 1.75 m in the morning. He gets out of the hole that day.
    1.75/(1/8) = 14 and 14 + 1 more day = 15 days.
13. b
14. (given)
15. h
16. i
    7 (days) x $191,781 (per day) = $1,342,467
17. 24,000 kilometers/32 kilometers per gallon = 750 gallons in 1 year
    750 gallons x .05 = 37.5 gallons
    You could save 37.5 gallons in 1 year.
18. Convert the 5 pounds into ounces by multiplying 5 pounds by 16 ounces (1 pound). Five pounds is 80 ounces. There are 8 families. 80/8 is 10.
    Each family gets 10 ounces of cheese.
19. 1 billion seconds x 1 min/60 sec = 16,666,667 minutes
    16,666,667 minutes x 1 hour/60 min = 277,778 hours
    277,778 hours x 1 day/24 hours = 11,574 days
    11,574 days x 1 year/365 days = 32 years.
    A billion seconds is 32 years old.
20. 1 hour 10 minutes is 70 minutes.
    28 seedlings ÷ 40 min = .7 of a seedling per minute
    .7 of a seedling x 70 minutes = 49 seedlings

Pages 14–16

1. d
2. g
3. (given)
4. l
   9:00 A.M. – (15 minutes + 20 minutes + 35 minutes)
   9:00 A.M. – 70 minutes, or 1 hour 10 minutes = 7:50 A.M.
5. c
6. h
7. (given)
8. l
   85 ÷ 2 = 42.5, but page numbers go in order; pages 42 and 43
9. d
10. h
11. k
12. n
13. b
14. (given)
15. h
16. k
    1 + 3 + 5 + 7 + 9 + 11 + 13 + 15 = 64 strawberries
    64 + 8 (taken out earlier) = 72 strawberries at the start
17. d
18. e
19. i
20. o
    3 trips with 10 cars + 2 trips with 6 trucks
    30 cars + 12 trucks = 42 vehicles

Pages 19 and 20

1. 540 minutes
2. 1,000 – 1,200 people
3. front-end estimation
4. compatible numbers
5. $9,000 – $11,000
6. a. greater
   b. Henry 240; April 210; Felicia 260
   c. April and Felicia
   d. 115 and 120
7. 730
8. $1,000 – $1,200
9. front-end estimation
10. 700 (by rounding down)
11. 412 + 629 ~ 1000
    325 + 685 ~ 1000
    879 ~ 900
    estimate: 2,900
12. 1,400 – 1,600
13. Colleen 8, Andrea 5
14. 13 paved, 8 unpaved

Pages 22–24

1. d
2. h
3. i
4. m
5. c
6. g
7. (1,000 x 3/4) – 200 = 550
8. j
   3/4 of 1000 is 750 cars in on Tuesday. 750 cars – 200 compact cars = 550 standard-size cars
9. d
10. f
11. (given)
12. j
    t (time) = 1.0 miles (distance) ÷ 1/5 mile per min (rate) = 5 min
13. b
14. h
15. i
16. m
17. b
18. e
19. i
20. o
    If it costs 77 cents to produce 35 cars, then each car costs: 77/35 = 2.2 cents. It costs 2.2 cents to make each car. So 385 cars x 2.2 cents for each car = 847 cents, or $8.47 to produce 385 cars.

Page 28

1. 2 1/2 cookies each
2. $55.75
3. $14,756.75
4. $148.00
5. 16
6. 50, 100
7. 68
8. 225
9. $50
10. $32.50

Pages 30–32

1. First column 4 = 2 + 2
   2 x 2 = 4
   Second column 5 = 2 + 3
   2 x 3 = 6

4	5	9	**13**	**10**	**15**	16	**3**	7
2	2	4	**7**	5	7	**7**	1	**3**
2	3	5	6	**5**	8	**9**	2	4
4	6	20	42	25	**56**	63	2	12

2. 1,2 2,3 3,4 4,5 5,6 6,7 7,8 8,9
   1,3 2,4 3,5 4,6 5,7 6,8 7,9
   1,4 2,5 3,6 4,7 5,8 6,9
   1,5 2,6 3,7 4,8 5,9
   1,6 2,7 3,8 4,9
   1,7 2,8 3,9
   1,8 2,9
   1,9
   36 = 8 + 7 + 6 + 5 + 4 + 3 + 2 + 1

   There are 36 children.
3. a. 2 + 4 + 6 + 8 + 10 + 12 + 14 + 16 + 18 + 20 + 22 + 24 = $156.00

   b. $8190.00
4. .01 +.02 +.04 +.08 +.16 +.32 +.64 = $1.27 > $1.25

   Rob should ask for a daily allowance.
5. Every 7 days it's another Tuesday. So start by dividing 100 by 7 to get 14 with a remainder of 2. So in 100 days, 14 Tuesdays will go by + 2 extra days, making it Thursday.
6.

Renters	Kilowatt Hours
1	2
2	5
3	7
4	10
5	12
6	15
7	17
8	20
9	22
10	25

7. 320
8. 50 minutes
9. August 9th
10. Each member in the series is the sum of the two numbers before it.

    The next numbers are 377, 610, 987
11. East! It always points east at a quarter past.
12.

15	1	2	12
4	10	9	7
8	6	5	11
3	13	14	0

13. Between the first and second numbers is a difference of 2. Between the second and third, a difference of 4. Between the third and fourth, a difference of 6. And so on. If the pattern were to continue, the next number would be a difference of 8—and 20 valentines would have been exchanged.
14. The first two lines have eight syllables each; the next two have 6 each, and the last line has nine. Also, the 1st, 2nd, and last lines rhyme with each other, and the 3rd and 4th rhyme, too.
15. 10 + 9 + 8 + 7 = 34 cans

Pages 34 and 35

1. a. 21 m; 9.5 m^2
   b. 12 m; 9 m^2
   c. 54 m; 81 m^2
   d. 162 m
2. a. 177 mL
   b. 946 mL
   c. 473 mL
   d. 473 mL
   e. 1.89 mL
3. a. 84 $ft.^2$
   b. 336 $ft.^2$
   c. 4 quarts
4. Buy by quarts. 1 gallon = 3.25 x 4 = $13.00
5. a. He has grown six inches in the last three years.
   60 inches = 5 feet
   63 inches = 5 feet and three inches
   b. 66 inches = 5 feet and six inches
6. a. Tom, Mary, Paula, and Sam
   b. Sam—167 cm
   Paula—157 cm
   Mary—152 cm
   Tom—147 cm
7. 480 mL
8. one teaspoon of salt
   1/2 x 2 = 1
9. a. .36 feet
   b. 432 inches
10. 36 inches = 1 yard, 3 yards = 36 + 36 + 36 = 108 inches
11. 4 boxes will cover 80 feet, 20 x 4 = 80
12. 15 inches
13. 5 lbs.
14. 7 lbs.
15. 2 tons
16. 2 cups
17. 4 pints
18. 16 jars
19. yes
20. Tom, (3.12 miles = 5 km)

Pages 37–39

1. 4 pieces
2. 2 1/2 quarts; no
3. $ 2.00
4. a. $ .40
   b. $ .50
5. $609.44
6. $417.30
7. $90.62
8. $19.33
9. $56.55
10. $1.26
11. $0.04
12. 16
13. no; less (1/5)
14. Paul: $6.00, Todd: $7.25, Eli $5.00; total: $18.25
15. $16.00; $32.00
16. 12, 15, 3
17. $31,250
18. 35.95 inches
19. 6 tries
20. 489 divided by 6 equals 81 with a remainder of 3. He can sell 81 bunches, which would leave him 3 to sell at the regular price.
21. $6 per hour
22. 35 lbs. per box
23. 38 hours; $266
24. b; $58
25. d. 360 lbs.
26. 10 P.M. is 9 hours later. If the clock loses 3 minutes every hour, it will be 27 minutes behind or 9:33 P.M. when it is supposed to read 10 P.M.
27. Number of houses = $4,608/$256 per house = 18 houses
28. $0.23 is spent on the peel.
    $1.80 – $0.23 = $1.57 on banana
29. James spent $37.42; he saved $12.48
30. Laurel paid $13.50 for the gift. Joey paid $9.00 for the gift.

Pages 40 and 41

1. $24
2. play
3. movie
4. concert
5. $2
6. $60
7. fifth graders
8. Mon. – Fri., 8 –11 P.M.
9. Sat., 7 A.M. – 1 P.M.
10. 500 glasses
11. 350 glasses
12. 50 glasses
13. 1,100 glasses
14. 19%
15. 62%
16. 81%
17. deer and squirrels
18. more

Pages 42–44

Frog Race

Frog 1 = 65 seconds
Frog 2 = 68 seconds
Frog 1 wins the race.

Bad Dogs!

2 hours (1:00 A.M.)

Free Dinner

5 dinners

Race to Rescue

Joshua will reach his father first.

At the rate of 22 miles per hour, Benjamin's raft covers the distance of 40 miles in 40 ÷ 22 = 1.8 hours. Adding the time for three delays, 3 x 0.4 = 1.2 hours, his total time is 3 hours.

Thirty percent of Joshua's 32-mile trail (or 32 x 0.3 = 9.6 miles) is steep, and at a rate of 8 miles per hour, he covers this steep section in 9.6 ÷ 8 = 1.2 hours. At a rate of 15 miles per hour on the 22.4 mile flat section, Joshua covers this in 22.4 ÷ 15 = 1.5 hours. His total time is 2.7 hours.

At her average rate of 5 miles per hour, Hannah covers her 14 mile mountain trail in 14 ÷ 5 = 2.8 hours, but her rest time at the summit takes 10 ÷ 60 or nearly 0.2 hours, so her total time, like Benjamin's, is 3 hours.

Their father rides Joshua's horse back to the village and treats the child.

Clever Math Teachers

Mr. Ric Tangle is in school, while Mr. Perry Meter, Mr. Sol Ution, Ms. Dee Nominator, and Mr. Cal Culator are not.

Mr. Perry Meter is not at school. There are four 12's on one side of the equation and 5 on the other.

Mr. Ric Tangle is at school. The commutative property of numbers tells us that it doesn't matter what order the numbers are in when you multiply.

Ms. Py R. Square is at school. 50 x 30 would be 1,500, so 50 x 32 must be > 1,000.

Mr. Sol Ution is not at school. 1/4 + 1/4 = 1/2, not 1/8.

Ms. Dee Nominator is not at school. The two numbers on the left of the equal sign are not quite the same as the two numbers on the right.

Mr. Cal Culator is at not at school. If 33 + z = 107, z = 107 – 33, which is 74, not 64.

At the Corner Store

The prices are: $1.20, $1.25, $1.50, and $3.16

Bare Feet

12 – 7 = 5 people in bare feet!

Two Trains Running

At time t, the distance the passenger train is from the terminal is d = 50t. At this same time, the distance the freight train is from the terminal is d = 30(t + 1). The t + 1 is because at any given time t, the freight train has been traveling an hour longer than the second train. They pass each other when their two distances are the same, or 30(t + 1) = 50t. Solve for t to get 3/2 or 1.5 hours. The trains will pass each other after 1.5 hours.

Sheep or Kids?

There are two possible answers: 1 person and 2 sheep or 3 people and 1 sheep.

The Airplane and the Square

Side	Time (min)
1.	60
2.	30
3.	20
4.	15

Total = 2 hrs. 5 min. = 25/12 hrs
Average speed = 400 miles ÷ (25/12) hrs = 192 mph

 © Teacher Created Resources, Inc.